38.95

BS
2589
.S776
2003

Journal of Pentecostal Theology

Supplement Series
16

Editors
John Christopher Thomas
Rickie D. Moore
Steven J. Land

Sheffield Academic Press
Sheffield

The Prophethood

of All Believers

A Study in Luke's Charismatic Theology

Roger Stronstad

Sheffield Academic Press

To Michael Szuk
Diane Vint
and Jamie and Carrie McDonald:
former students, friends

First published 1999
Reprinted 2003, 2004
Copyright © 1999, 2003 Sheffield Academic Press
A Continuum imprint

Published by Sheffield Academic Press Ltd
The Tower Building, 11 York Road, London SE1 7NX
15 East 26th Street, Suite 1703, New York NY 10010

www.continuumbooks.com

All rights reserved. No part of this publication may be reproduced or transmitted in any form or by any means, electronic or mechanical, including photocopying, recording or any information storage or retrieval system, without permission in writing from the publishers.

British Library Cataloguing-in-Publication Data
A catalogue record for this book is available from the British Library

Typeset by Sheffield Academic Press
Printed on acid-free paper in Great Britain by CPI Bath

ISBN 1-84127-005-9

CONTENTS

ACKNOWLEDGMENTS

Several people have contributed to the production of this book. D.J. Groen and Judy Cathers typed the four original lectures, which are herein revised as Chapters 2–5. Jamie McDonald and Michael Szuk have given invaluable computer assistance to me.

Western Pentecostal Bible College gave me sabbatical time (January–June 1998) to complete the writing of this manuscript, which had been set aside since 1993. The Association of Canadian Bible Colleges awarded me a research grant to help cover research costs.

Dr David Wenham, Wycliffe Hall, Oxford, has read the manuscript and offered constructive criticism. This has been especially helpful since he disagrees with my interpretation at a number of key points.

I would like to thank the above persons and institutions for the assistance, support and encouragement which they have extended to me.

Abbotsford, British Columbia
30 June 1998

ABBREVIATIONS

AB	Anchor Bible
CBL	The Complete Biblical Library
HNTC	Harper's NT Commentaries
ICC	International Critical Commentary
JPT	*Journal of Pentecostal Theology*
JPTSup	*Journal of Pentecostal Theology*, Supplement Series
JSNT	*Journal for the Study of the New Testament*
JSNTSup	*Journal for the Study of the New Testament*, Supplement Series
LSJ	H.G. Liddell, Robert Scott and H. Stuart Jones, *Greek–English Lexicon* (Oxford: Clarendon Press, 9th edn, 1968)
NAC	The New American Commentary
NCB	New Century Bible
NIBC	New International Biblical Commentary
NICNT	New International Commentary on the New Testament
NIGTC	The New International Greek Testament Commentary
RCNT	The Radiant Commentary on the New Testament
TDNT	Gerhard Kittel and Gerhard Friedrich (eds.), *Theological Dictionary of the New Testament* (trans. Geoffrey W. Bromiley; 10 vols.; Grand Rapids: Eerdmans, 1964–)
TNTC	Tyndale New Testament Commentaries
WBC	Word Biblical Commentary

INTRODUCTION

The following study returns to and develops the subject about which I first wrote in the short, popular article 'Prophets and Pentecost', in *The Pentecostal Testimony* (March 1976, p. 5). In its present form this book had its impetus in the invitation to give the inaugural Pentecostal lectureship at Asia Pacific Theological Seminary, Baguio City, Philippines, in February 1993. Chapters 2–5, inclusive, update and revise those lectures.

The style of discussion reflects the fact that at its heart it contains four updated and revised lectures. Graduate students, academics, pastors and missionaries made up its first audience. The presentation necessarily reflected the limitations which are inherent in a public lecture to a diverse audience. For example, it lacks the characteristic comprehensiveness of a thesis or dissertation. It also lacks the scholarly sophistication of a formal research project. I have written this book for a similarly mixed readership—undergraduate and graduate students, academics, the clergy and interested and informed laypeople. Just as the original lectures were written to be listened to, so this book is written to be read (and not just used for research purposes). To this end I have steered the course between unhelpful brevity, on the one hand, and tedious lengthiness, on the other hand; between being too popular and too technical.

This study is not about 'the theology of St Luke'. It is much more narrowly focused. It examines the data in Luke–Acts about Jesus, the fountainhead of Christianity, and about his disciples and their converts and their individual and corporate experience of the Holy Spirit. Many important and relevant data, such as those, for example, about Jesus as the royal Messiah, Jesus' teaching about the kingdom of God, and his radical ministry to the marginalized, are discussed only as they intersect the data about Jesus as the eschatological anointed prophet, and the disciples as a community of Spirit-baptized prophets. To discuss Luke's data about Jesus as the royal Messiah and other Lukan themes more fully would shift the focus of this study and, indeed, make it a very different kind of book.

In studying Luke's data about 'the prophethood of all believers', I have tried to think Luke's thoughts after him. Of course, every interpreter gives lip service to this aim. But the literature in this field, with its often diverse and mutually contradictory interpretations, shows that many interpreters fail to meet this aim. For example, in spite of the fact that there is a widespread consensus in academia that each biblical author is to be interpreted in his own right and on his own terms, it still remains a commonplace to read Luke through Pauline glasses. James D.G. Dunn was guilty of this in his 1970 benchmark study, *Baptism in the Holy Spirit*.[1] In spite of significant criticism leveled against him for doing this, in a response to his critics some two decades later he still insists 'that the pneumatology of Luke is essentially one with the pneumatology of Paul'.[2]

I have interpreted Luke–Acts independently of the other Gospels and the epistles. Nevertheless, where I have judged it to be appropriate, I have sometimes turned to the other Gospels, largely to Matthew, to illustrate some aspect of Luke's distinctive report about Jesus. Similarly, I have also turned to Paul's epistles, specifically to 1 Thessalonians and 1 Corinthians, to illustrate the selective character of Luke's narrative strategy. But in *illustrating* some aspect of Luke's data from Matthew's Gospel or Paul's epistles I have avoided *interpreting* Luke as though he were either Matthew or Paul.

In regards to the subject of this study, namely, 'the prophethood of all believers', my aim of thinking Luke's thoughts after him is to understand the meaning of Spirit-baptism and its relationship to either salvation or to vocation. When reading Luke–Acts I have observed that Luke often explicitly relates the presence and activity of the Holy Spirit to vocation as the Spirit of prophecy. I have also observed that Luke, in contrast to both John and Paul, never explicitly reports that the Holy Spirit effects salvation. I do find several ambiguous texts, most notably Acts 2.38, 39 and Acts 11.15-17, which some interpreters interpret soteriologically and others interpret vocationally. In light of these observations—namely (1) Luke often explicitly relates the Spirit to vocation; and (2) he never unambiguously describes the Spirit to be the

1.   London: SCM Press.

2.   James D.G. Dunn, 'Baptism in the Holy Spirit: A Response to Pentecostal Scholarship on Luke–Acts', *JPT* 3 (1993), pp. 3-27 (27).

agent of salvation—I have consistently interpreted the problematic, ambiguous texts vocationally rather than soteriologically. Thus, I have interpreted Acts 2.38, 39 to mean that salvation is the prerequisite to receiving the promised gift of the Spirit of prophecy, and that the gift of the Spirit of prophecy which was received by Cornelius is identical to the vocational gift of the Spirit which was poured out on the disciples on the day of Pentecost. But other interpreters insist that these texts be interpreted soteriologically.[3] Each interpreter needs to be true, not, of course, to himself or herself, but to what Luke actually wrote (and not to what they wish or imagine he wrote). Readers of this book must judge for themselves whether or not the interpretation which I offer in this study is true to what Luke actually wrote.

The book unfolds in the following way. Chapter 1 offers some guidelines and principles about reading, interpreting and applying Luke–Acts as historical narrative. Chapter 2 examines both Jesus' experience of the Spirit and his teaching and announcements about the Spirit (Luke 1–24). Chapter 3 analyzes Luke's report about the transformation of the disciples from frightened followers to a Spirit-baptized, Spirit-empowered and Spirit-filled community of prophets (Acts 1.12–2.41). Chapter 4 surveys the acts and the witness of this community of prophets in Jerusalem (Acts 2.42–6.7). Chapter 5 focuses on Luke's report about the acts of five charismatic prophets, namely, Stephen in Jerusalem, Philip in Samaria, Barnabas and Agabus in Syrian Antioch, and Peter in western Judea (Acts 6.8–12.24). Chapter 6 is about the acts of the charismatic prophet, Paul (Acts 12.25–28.31). Finally, Chapter 7 synthesizes Luke's data about the prophethood of all believers and briefly offers some suggestions about the relevance of the doctrine of the prophethood of all believers for contemporary Christianity.

---

3. Dunn, 'Baptism in the Holy Spirit', p. 26; Max Turner, *Power from on High: The Spirit in Israel's Restoration and Witness in Luke–Acts* (JPTSup, 9; Sheffield: Sheffield Academic Press, 1996), p. 39.

Chapter 1

READING, INTERPRETING AND APPLYING LUKE–ACTS

Within the literature of the New Testament Luke–Acts has several distinguishing characteristics. Along with Mark, upon which it is based, and Matthew, with which it shares many additional data, Christians traditionally classify Luke as one of the synoptic Gospels. It is, however, the only self-consciously written, self-designated historical narrative in the New Testament. Thus, whereas Mark designates his book about Jesus as a 'gospel' (εὐαγγελίον [Mk 1.1]) Luke designates part one of his two-volume book as a historical narrative (διήγησιν [Lk. 1.1], λόγον [Acts 1.1]). Therefore, to whatever extent Luke borrows from the Gospels, such as Mark and Matthew, he has transformed his report about Jesus into a historical narrative. In fact, the book which bears his name has as much in common with the sacred historiography of ancient Israel, and even with the secular historiography of the Greco-Roman world, as it does with the other Gospels.

The book of Luke is also the only book in the New Testament to be written with a sequel, namely, the Acts of the Apostles. In fact, Luke and Acts are the first and second accounts, that is, the first and second scrolls of the single hyphenated book which we call Luke–Acts. In writing Acts as the sequel to his first account about the origins of the gospel Luke did what neither Mark, nor Matthew, nor John thought it necessary to do. Because he wrote Acts as the necessary sequel to his first account, Luke's two-volume history about the origin and the spread of Christianity (Luke–Acts) is at one and the same time: (1) the longest book in the New Testament; and (2) the largest part of the New Testament. No other writer, not even Paul, has written as much of the New Testament as Luke wrote.

Clearly, this unique and lengthy historical narrative presents the interpreter with a wide-ranging, complex set of interpretive challenges. In this chapter I will discuss the following subjects: (1) reading Luke–Acts; (2) interpreting Luke–Acts; and (3) applying Luke–Acts. This discussion forms the foundation for the following exposition of Luke's doctrine of the people of God as the prophethood of all believers (Chapters 2–7).

1. *Reading Luke–Acts*

Reading historical narrative, specifically, Luke–Acts, is not simply like reading other biblical literature, such as the Law, the Psalms, the epistles or the Apocalypse. Reading Luke–Acts requires a distinctive set of skills and literary sensibilities. To read Luke–Acts as more than mere story the reader must be alert to the way Luke has structured his two-part narrative and be alert to the narrative strategies which he employs. These narrative strategies include, but are not limited to: (1) programmatic episodes; (2) inclusio; and (3) parallelism.

1.1. *The Structure of Luke–Acts*

Arguably, Luke–Acts is the most carefully designed book in all of biblical literature, certainly, in the New Testament. For example, both parts of his book (i.e. Luke–Acts) have the following thematic elements: (1) a 'beginning' narrative; (2) an inauguration narrative, which contains reports about the gift of the Holy Spirit and an accompanying sermon which explains that gift; (3) reports of confirmatory miracles and the complementary approval/disapproval response theme; (4) a travel narrative; and (5) a trials narrative.

The obvious parallels in the structure between Luke and Acts are not a mere happenstance. They are the product of Luke's careful and skillful design. Luke selected his data, both by inclusion and exclusion, so that the structure of Acts parallels the structure of its predecessor, Luke. This observation about the parallel structure of the two volumes is confirmed by observing that, on a smaller scale, Luke reports each of Paul's three evangelistic tours according to the same structure: (1) introductory episode(s); (2) a major report about one city; and (3) a series of summary reports. The chart on p. 15 illustrates the common structure to be found in Luke's reports about Paul's three evangelistic tours.

These parallels between the structures of Luke and Acts, on the one hand, and between Paul's three evangelistic tours, on the other hand, show Luke to be a careful, highly skilled narrator.

Tour	Introductory Episodes	Major Report (Focus)	Series of Summary Reports
1	Emphasis is on the initiative of the Holy Spirit (13.1-3)	Pisidian Antioch (13.13-52)	Tour resumes and concludes in Antioch, with an aftermath in Jerusalem (14.1–15.30)
2	Emphasis is on the leading of the Holy Spirit (16.6-8)	Philippi (16.11-40)	Tour resumes and concludes in Antioch, with an appendix about Apollos (17.1–18.28)
3	Emphasis is on the gift of the Holy Spirit (19.1-7)	Ephesus (19.8-41)	Tour resumes and concludes in Jerusalem (20.1–22.21)

1.2. *The Narrative Strategies*

Luke incorporates programmatic episodes into his narrative strategy for his successive reports about Jesus and his disciples. Luke's report about Jesus' baptism through to his complementary explanatory sermon in the synagogue in Nazareth is programmatic for his public ministry. From the first Luke shows Jesus to be the Spirit-anointed, Spirit-ful, Spirit-led and Spirit-empowered eschatological prophet. What is true at the beginning of his public ministry is also true for his entire ministry which follows. Lest any readers either fail to observe the programmatic function of the inauguration narrative or lose sight of it Luke gives them periodic reminders. For example, he reports: that Jesus performed empowered works (Lk. 5.17); that people recognize that Jesus is a great prophet (Lk. 7.16); that Jesus teaches about the Holy Spirit (Lk. 11.13; 12.11, 12); that Jesus instructs by the Spirit (Acts 1.2); and, finally, that Jesus pours out the Spirit upon his disciples (Acts 2.33). Similarly, because Jesus transferred the Spirit from himself to his disciples on the day of Pentecost, the Pentecost narrative is programmatic for their ongoing ministry in the Spirit. In other words, from the day of Pentecost onwards they are the eschatological community of Spirit-baptized, Spirit-empowered and Spirit filled prophets. The programmatic function of the Pentecost narrative is amply reinforced by Luke's frequent reports about the prophetic activity of the disciples (and their converts).

In Luke's narrative strategy his programmatic narratives are, by their very nature, comparatively rare. He uses another narrative strategy, called inclusio, much more frequently. Inclusio is the strategy which brackets a narrative with either similar episodes or terminology. The opening episode or term is programmatic for what follows. The closing bracket is retrospective, reminding the reader about the theme, while at the same time cutting it off. Luke uses inclusio both on the large scale and on the small scale. His portrait of Jesus as the eschatological anointed prophet is an example of inclusio on a large scale. In Lk. 4.18-21 Luke introduces Jesus as the Spirit-anointed prophet who fulfills the mission of the Isaianic prophet (Isa. 61.1). He next reports that Jesus identifies himself as a prophet whose ministry of turning from his own people to others echoes the prophets Elijah and Elisha who turned from Israel to minister to Gentiles (Lk. 4.22-27). Finally, he reports that Jesus' townspeople reject their native son, and, indeed, attempt to kill him (Lk. 4.28-30)—the punishment meted out to a false prophet. This cluster of episodes (Lk. 4.16-30) is the opening bracket in the strategy of inclusio, identifying Jesus as prophet. The closing bracket is the retrospective description of Jesus as a prophet powerful in works and word, but rejected by the leaders of Israel (Lk. 24.19, 20). The function of this inclusio is to inform Luke's readers that Jesus is the eschatological anointed prophet from first (Lk. 4) to last (Lk. 24).

Luke also uses inclusio on a smaller scale. For example, he initially describes Stephen as 'a man full of faith and of the Holy Spirit' (Acts 6.5). He concludes his brief report about Stephen by describing him as being 'full of the Holy Spirit' (Acts 7.55). In this way Luke defines Stephen's 'wonders and signs' (Acts 6.8), his witness (Acts 6.9-14) and his defense before the Sanhedrin (Acts 7.1-53) to be the works and words of a Spirit-ful prophet from first to last. There are many other examples of inclusio as well, not least of which are Luke's references to the Holy Spirit which introduce each of Paul's three evangelistic tours with the introductory references to the second and third evangelistic tours forming an inclusio with the introductory references to the first and second tours, respectively.

Readers of Luke–Acts have long observed that Luke often uses the narrative strategy of parallelism. This parallelism, as we have demonstrated, begins with the parallel structure of Luke and Acts. It includes parallels between Jesus' experience of the Spirit and his disciples' subsequent experience of the Spirit. The parallels are as follows: (1) just as Jesus begins his ministry anointed by the Spirit (Lk. 3.22/4.18), so the disciples will not begin their ministry until they have been baptized with the Spirit (Acts 1.4, 5); (2) just as Jesus is full of the Holy Spirit (Lk. 4.1a), so the disciples will be filled with the Holy Spirit (Acts 2.4); just as Jesus is led by the Spirit (Lk. 4.1b), so disciples such as Philip, Peter and Paul, respectively, will be led by the Spirit (Acts 8.29; 10.19;

16.6, 7, etc.); and just as Jesus is empowered by the Spirit (Lk. 4.14), with the result that he performs miracles, wonders and signs (Acts 2.22), so the apostles, Peter, Stephen, Philip, and Barnabas and Paul will also perform wonders and signs (Acts 2.43; 5.12; 6.8; 8.6, 13; 14.3). This parallelism shows that because Jesus has transferred the Spirit of prophecy from himself to his disciples they will have, both as a community and as individuals, the same kind of prophetic ministry as he himself had.

Luke portrays Stephen as the most Christ-like figure in his lengthy narrative. He reports Stephen's experience of the Holy Spirit and complementary Spirit-ful ministry to be parallel to Jesus' experience of the Spirit and complementary ministry, in ways including, but not limited to, the following parallels. Both Jesus and Stephen are full of the Holy Spirit (Lk. 4.1a; Acts 6.5; 7.55). Further, Jesus increases in wisdom and Stephen is full of wisdom (Lk. 2.52; Acts 6.3, 10). Both are accused of blasphemy (Lk. 5.21; Acts 6.11). Both are also accused of speaking against the temple (Lk. 21.6; Acts 6.13). Moreover, both die as rejected prophets (Lk. 24.19, 20; Acts 7.51-53). Finally, both pray for their murderers (Lk. 23.34; Acts 7.60). These and other points of similarity between Jesus and Stephen highlight their unique positions in the unfolding of salvation history. It is through Jesus' ministry and death as the rejected prophet that the provision of salvation is made; it is through Stephen's ministry and death as a rejected prophet that Christianity begins its decisive break with Judaism and salvation begins to be taken to Samaria and, ultimately, to the Gentiles.

As Luke reports it, Paul's experience of the Spirit and complementary ministry often mirror Peter's. For example, as individuals and as members of a group both Peter and Paul are filled with the Holy Spirit three times (Acts 2.4; 4.8, 31; 9.17; 13.9, 52). They are also led by the Spirit (e.g. Acts 10.19; 13.2-4; 16.6, 7). Both Peter and Paul minister to Gentiles and are severely criticized for doing so (Acts 10.1 11.18; 13.1–15.38). Both perform signs and wonders (Acts 5.12; 14.3), which include healing the lame (Acts 3.1-10; 9.32-35; 14.8-10), and raising the dead (Acts 9.36-43; 20.9-12). At the very least Luke reports these parallels between Paul and Peter to establish Paul's credentials as an authentic, legitimate Spirit-filled apostle-prophet in spite of his radically different history than the other apostle-prophets, such as Peter's.

Clearly, in writing his two-volume history about Jesus, the eschatological anointed prophet, and the disciples and their converts as communities of Spirit-baptized prophets, Luke did not simply string together events in a random, haphazard way. The parallel structure of his two volumes shows that consciously and carefully he crafted his narrative about the origin of Christianity in Galilee and Judea and its spread from Jerusalem to Samaria and Judea and to the ends of the earth. Narrative strategies, such as programmatic episodes, inclusio and parallelism reinforce this picture of Luke as the most skillful of word-smiths.

2. *Interpreting Luke–Acts*

Interpreting Luke's narrative of history (Luke–Acts) is not simply like interpreting the imperatives of the Law, the laments or praises of the Psalms, the circumstantial instructions of the epistles, or like decoding the visions of the Apocalypse. In addition to the hermeneutical princi-ples which are common to the interpretation of all biblical literature, irrespective of genre, interpreting Luke–Acts brings into play its own set of guidelines. These include, but are not limited to: (1) observing that Luke–Acts is selective history; (2) setting Luke–Acts into the his-torical context of Greco-Roman history; and (3) observing Luke's mul-tiplex historical-didactic-theological purpose.

That art/science of interpretation which we call hermeneutics has three elements. First, there is the range of presuppositions which every interpreter brings to the task of interpreting the text. Secondly, there are those principles which guide the interpreter in the task of exegesis. Thirdly, there are those principles which guide the interpreter in apply-ing the text to contemporary Christian living. In the discussion which follows, I will assume the hermeneutical model which generally charac-terizes an evangelical Protestant interpretation of the Bible. However, because I am interpreting Luke–Acts, a text which bears special signifi-cance for my experience as a Pentecostal, and, further, because the text is historical narrative, a genre over which there is much controversy concerning its didactic role, I will briefly summarize some points that are particularly relevant to my exposition of Luke's doctrine of the people of God as the prophethood of all believers.

2.1. *Presuppositions*
Whether he or she is aware of it or not every interpreter brings a variety of experiential, rational and spiritual presuppositions to the interpreta-tion of the Scriptures. In particular, the Pentecostal interpreter, such as

myself, brings his or her own experience of being filled with the Spirit as a presupposition to Luke's report that on the day of Pentecost the disciples 'were filled with the Holy Spirit and began to speak with other tongues as the Spirit gave utterance' (Acts 2.4), and believes that he or she is justified in understanding the experience of the disciples in the light of his or her own similar experience. Further presuppositions are pertinent to the study of Acts: first, that Luke's pneumatology is influenced by the charismatic pneumatology of the Old Testament as it is mediated to him through LXX;[1] secondly, that the two books, Luke and Acts, were written and published together as a literary unit, and, therefore (1) each book is the same genre, namely, historical narrative (διήγησιν, Lk. 1.1);[2] and (2) despite the historical particularity of each book they have a common, homogenous theological perspective.

2.2. *Guidelines for Interpreting Luke–Acts*

For the interpretation of Luke–Acts, three guidelines need to be noted: (1) Luke–Acts is selective history; (2) Luke–Acts must be set in the historical, political, social and religious context of the Greco-Roman world; and (3) Luke has a multiplex purpose in writing Luke–Acts.

2.2.1. *Luke–Acts is Selective History.* Like his predecessors and mentors, the editors and chroniclers of the sacred history of the Jews, Luke makes no attempt to give his patron, Theophilus (Lk. 1.1-4; Acts 1.1-2), and all subsequent readers of his two books a complete history about either Jesus, the apostles and their fellow workers, or about the origin and spread of the gospel. Rather, from out of his own participation in some of the events which he has recorded (note the 'we' passages beginning at Acts 16.10), and also from out of the vast pool of information which he has gathered, he gives his readers a select history which reflects and supports the parallel structure of his two volumes and, also,

---

1. Roger Stronstad, 'The Influence of the Old Testament on the Charismatic Theology of St Luke', *Pneuma* 2.1 (1980): pp. 28-50, (32-50); *idem, The Charismatic Theology of St Luke* (Peabody, MA: Hendrickson, 1984), pp. 17-20.

2. Contra Gordon D. Fee and Douglas Stuart, *How to Read the Bible for All its Worth: A Guide to Understanding the Bible* (Grand Rapids: Zondervan, 1982), p. 90. Fee writes, 'Acts is the only one of its kind in the New Testament'. This is an astonishing statement from a champion of 'genre' hermeneutics. It is astonishing because Luke's term διήγησιν/narrative (Lk. 1.1) applies to his entire two-volume history. Thus, Luke is not one kind of genre and Acts a second kind of genre—the only one of its kind in the New Testament.

is related to the multiplex purpose which governs his writing. Undoubtedly, Luke knows much more than he writes. And yet, in comparison to both the Gospels and the epistles, he sometimes tells more than the others. Because Luke is the most prolific writer in the New Testament and the data are so immense, illustrations of the selective character of Luke–Acts must be limited to a few examples.

A comparison of Luke's 'first book' with the Gospels written by Matthew, Mark and John shows that Luke has included much distinctive material which the others do not. For example, Luke's infancy narrative (Lk. 1.5–2.52) has few parallels with Matthew's infancy narrative (Mt. 1.18–2.33) and has none with either Mark's or John's Gospels, because both those lack an infancy narrative. Further, Luke's so-called 'travel narrative' (Lk. 9.5–19.27) contains much exclusive material, including the report of the mission of the 70 (Lk. 10.1-24), and a number of parables, such as the parable of the Good Samaritan (Lk. 10.25-37). In addition, Luke's resurrection narrative is notoriously independent of the reports of the other Gospels containing, for example, the episode of Jesus' resurrection appearance to the two disciples on the road to Emmaus (Lk. 24.13-35), and Jesus' promise of the divine empowering which awaited the disciples in Jerusalem (Lk. 24.49).

Not only does Luke include many independent and exclusive data, Luke's selection is also evident by what he excludes from his narrative, whether or not this exclusion is a factor of the limited nature of his data, or whether it is a matter of his editorial strategy. For example, Luke's infancy narrative tells the reader little about the lives of Zacharias and Elizabeth, now aged and soon to be parents of John the Baptist, or of Mary and Joseph, the soon-to-be the earthly parents of Jesus, the Son of God. Further, with the exception of Jesus' visit to Jerusalem with his parents at age 12 (Lk. 2.41-51), Luke tells us nothing about his childhood, or early adult life prior to his baptism. It is the tantalizing silence on these and other matters in Luke and the other Gospels which in the end proved to be such a powerful motivation in the creation of the apocryphal infancy Gospels of the second and third centuries.

What is true of Luke's selectivity in writing his 'first book' is just as true for his writing of his sequel, the Acts of the Apostles. For example, of the 120 disciples, both men and women, who await the thrice promised gift of the Holy Spirit (Lk. 24.49; Acts 1.5, 8), Luke tells us nothing further about Mary, the mother of Jesus, or about the conversion and Christian lives of Jesus' brothers. James is the only exception to this, and he appears in the narrative but twice (Acts 15.12-21; 21.17-26). Luke tells his readers nothing about the Eleven (Acts 1.13), except briefly about James and John, and more extensively about Peter. He is silent on the history of Christianity in Galilee. In addition, he is silent about the charismatic, prophetic experience of the churches in Thessalonica and Corinth. Finally, about the spread of the gospel to the three leading cities of the Roman Empire, namely, Rome, Alexandria and Antioch, Luke only tells his readers of the spread of the gospel to Antioch. Alexandria never enters the focus of his interest, and Rome is the goal of Paul's ministry, which, when reached, brings his narrative to an end.

As limited as this brief survey is by space constraints, it clearly demonstrates the selectivity which Luke brought to the writing of his two volumes. Indeed, it is true that all historiography is necessarily selective and interpretive. And so it was for Luke when he wrote his report about the origin and spread of Christianity, just as it is for all historians, ancient and modern, sacred or secular. Both in what he includes in his narrative and what he excludes from his narrative, Luke reports only those sayings and events which conform to, advance and illustrate his purposes.

2.2.2. *Luke–Acts Must be Set in the Context of the Greco-Roman World.* Like the historians of Old Testament times who set the sacred history of Israel into the context of the political history of the nations of the ancient Near East, Luke set his narrative about the origin and spread of Christianity into the political, cultural and religious context of the Greco-Roman world, which, of course, includes Palestinian Judaism of the Second Temple period. Since Jesus and his disciples were Jews in Galilee and ministered almost exclusively among the Jews in Galilee and Judea, this, at first, may seem to be a matter to be disputed. However, this observation is validated, in part at least, by the fact that Jesus was born in Bethlehem of Judea as a result of a decree from Caesar Augustus for a census which required Joseph to visit his ancestral home (Lk. 2.1-7), and Jesus was executed under the authorization of Pontius Pilate, the Roman governor of Judea (Lk. 23.24), and by the hands of Roman soldiers (Lk. 23.33-38).

In events less dramatic than the birth and death of Jesus under Roman influence, the fledgling church, as reported by Luke, put its roots down in the far-flung, multinational soil of the Roman Empire. After the resurrection and ascension of Jesus, the disciples were initially restricted to Jerusalem and Judea, and were a sect within Judaism. Thus, the early Church initially had little direct contact with the Greco-Roman world. As reported by Luke, this changed primarily, though not exclusively, through Paul's evangelistic tours. For example, in Cyprus, where Barnabas and Saul began their peripatetic witness, they were summoned to appear before the proconsul, Sergius Paulus (Acts 13.7), who believed, being amazed at the teaching of the Lord (Acts 13.12). Somewhat later in Philippi, Paul and Silas were accused by its citizens of 'proclaiming customs which are not lawful for us to accept, being Romans' (Acts 16.21; note 16.37). Shortly thereafter in Thessalonica, Paul and Silas were accused of acting 'contrary to the decrees of Caesar' (Acts 17.7). Having traveled on from Thessalonica to Berea to Athens and then to Corinth, Paul met Aquila and Priscilla, who had been expelled from Rome (49 CE) when 'Claudius had commanded all the Jews to leave Rome' (Acts 18.2). In addition, while Paul was in Corinth, he was charged before the proconsul, Gallio, for persuading people to worship God in ways contrary to the Law (Acts 18.12-13). Since Gallio was appointed proconsul of Achaia in the summer of 51 CE, the interpreter has a fixed date to synchronize New Testament history with Roman history.

From Paul's witness to the non-Jewish peoples of Lystra, Athens and Ephesus (Acts 14.8-15; 17.16-34; 19.23-41) to his appeal to his Roman citizenship for protection and justice (e.g. Acts 16.37-40; 22.25-29; 25.10) and through to his arrest in Jerusalem and imprisonment and trials in Caesarea (Acts 21.27–26.32) and voyage to Rome (Acts 27–28), the interplay between Christianity and the Greco-Roman culture of the Mediterranean world steadily increases. Theophilus, and most other readers of Luke–Acts in the first century, would have understood this with little difficulty because it was part of their native experience. In contrast, the interpreter who studies Luke–Acts in the twentieth century must develop a working knowledge of the history and culture of the Greco-Roman world in order to understand it as its author intended.

2.2.3. *Luke–Acts Has a Multiplex Purpose.* It once was commonplace among interpreters to affirm that authorial intentionality, that is, the author's purpose for writing a document, is the essential criterion which governs the reader's understanding of the text.[3] But the question of

---

3.   G.D. Fee, 'Hermeneutics and Historical Precedent: A Major Problem in

authorial intentionality is complicated by a variety of factors. These include whether the purpose is explicit or implicit and whether it is simple or complex—that is, whether there is one primary purpose, or a combination of primary, secondary and even tertiary purposes. Consequently, several dangers attend the search to determine authorial intention. One danger is the all-too-common tendency toward reductionism, putting forward the claims of one purpose to the exclusion of all others. Another danger is to confuse the use to which the document, in whole or in part, might be put with the purpose of the document. The most insidious danger is to identify the interests and agenda of the interpreter as those of the author.

Luke–Acts is the longest document in the New Testament. It is also a two-part document with two successive but complementary foci. On the one hand, the first book focuses upon Jesus. Its setting is primarily the world of Judaism, and the subject is the origin of Christianity. On the other hand, the second book focuses on Jesus' disciples and their converts. Its setting progressively shifts from Judaism to the Greco-Roman world, and its subject is the spread of Christianity. Because of these factors, the question of Luke's purpose, as any survey of the relevant literature will show, is problematic.[4]

Though the question of Luke's purpose has proven to be problematic it is not a matter for despair. The most satisfactory answer to the question of Luke's purpose lies in the recognition that it is multiplex. This multiplex purpose not only has a historical dimension, as the reader would expect since the genre of Luke–Acts is historical narrative, but it also has both a didactic or instructional dimension and a theological dimension. Luke himself identifies this multiplex purpose, beginning with his prologue (Lk. 1.1-4).

In the prologue to his two-volume work, Luke identifies the genre of his writing. It is a διήγησιν (account, Lk. 1.1); it is also a λόγον (account, Acts 1.1). These terms identify Luke–Acts as historical narra

Pentecostal Hermeneutics', in Russell P. Spittler (ed.), *Perspectives on the New Pentecostalism* (Grand Rapids: Baker Book House, 1976), pp. 118-32 (125ff.); Fee and Stuart, *How to Read the Bible*, p. 89.

4.   Cf. Robert Maddox, *The Purpose of Luke–Acts* (Edinburgh: T. & T. Clark, 1982); W.W. Gasque, 'A Fruitful Field: Recent Study of the Acts of the Apostles', addendum to *idem*, *A History of the Interpretation of the Acts of the Apostles* (Peabody, MA: Hendrickson, 1980), pp. 342-59; and I. Howard Marshall, 'The Present State of Lukan Studies', *Themelios* 14.2 (1989), pp. 52-57.

tive. In identifying his documents as historical narrative, Luke immediately alerts his readers to the historical purpose of what he writes. As he informs his readers, this historical purpose relates to 'the things accomplished among us' (Lk. 1.1). These things begin with the birth announcements of John (Lk. 1.5-25) and Jesus (Lk. 1.26-38) and continue through to the two-year imprisonment of Paul in Rome (Acts 28.30-31)—events in which he was a sometime participant. Not only does he identify his genre as historical narrative but he also identifies his credentials; namely, that he has 'followed everything [either mentally or as a participant] from the beginning' (Lk. 1.3). Luke's historical purpose, then, is to narrate the events relating to the origin of Christianity and its spread in a sweep northwest to Rome.

Not only does Luke's multiplex purpose have a historical dimension, it also has a didactic or instructional dimension;[5] that is, he writes to instruct Theophilus and every other reader who will subsequently make up his audience. Specifically, he writes to bring Theophilus *et al.* to a reliable or exact knowledge of the truth of the things which have already been taught (Lk. 1.4). Thus, using the medium of historical narrative, Luke purposes to supply Theophilus with a more reliable instruction than that with which Theophilus's earlier instruction (κατηχήθης) had supplied him. If taken on his own terms, Luke makes a plain statement of his didactic intention. Clearly, as Luke practiced it, the writing of historical narrative was a medium and method of reliable instruction. Thus, as a historian Luke also saw himself as a teacher or instructor.

Using the genre, or medium, of historical narrative, Luke teaches Theophilus and his extended audience in a variety of ways. These include, but are not limited to: (1) proof from prophecy; (2) precedents and patterns; (3) reporting the teaching of Jesus; (4) reporting the teaching and preaching of apostles; and (5) using established theological terminology. First, Luke uses proof from prophecy periodically throughout his narrative. The two most important examples of proof from prophecy are to be found in his two inauguration narratives (i.e. Jesus' Nazareth address [Lk. 4.16-30], and the disciples' reception of the Holy Spirit [Acts 2.1-41]). In his Nazareth address Jesus reads a text from the prophet Isaiah (Isa. 61.1) and declares 'Today this Scripture has been

---

5. Fee minimizes the didactic purpose of Luke's narrative. He writes, 'for a Biblical precedent to justify a present action, the principles of the action must be taught elsewhere, where it is the primary intent so to teach' ('Hermeneutics', pp. 128-29); Fee and Stuart, *How to Read the Bible*, p. 101.

fulfilled in your hearing' (Lk. 4.21). Similarly, on the day of Pentecost Peter uses the pesher 'this is that' principle to interpret the pouring out of the Holy Spirit (Acts 2.2-4) with a text from the prophet Joel (Acts 2.17-21; Joel 2.28-32). And so, by including both the texts from Isaiah and Joel, respectively, Luke teaches that Jesus is the eschatological Spirit-anointed prophet and that subsequently his disciples become the eschatological community of Spirit-filled prophets.

In addition to teaching by proof from prophecy, Luke also teaches by precedents and patterns. For example, Peter's witness to Cornelius and his household (Acts 10.1-48) is the historical precedent which justifies the salvation of the Gentiles by grace apart from the works of the Law (Acts 15.6-11). This same episode also makes explicit the pattern for Spirit-baptism which Luke has earlier implied in his programmatic Pentecost narrative. The reception of the Spirit by Cornelius and his household (Acts 10.44-48) is the same experience as the disciples' reception of the Spirit on the day of Pentecost. Peter recognizes that they 'have received the Holy Spirit just as [we did]' (Acts 10.47). Later, he reports 'the Holy Spirit fell upon them, just as [He did] upon us at the beginning' (Acts 11.15), and, 'God therefore gave them the same gift as [He gave] to us' (Acts 11.17). Specifically, they were baptized with the Holy Spirit (Acts 11.16), and, as a result, they were 'speaking in tongues and exalting God' (Acts 10.46), by which 'God bore witness to them, giving them the Holy Spirit, just as He also did to us' (Acts 15.8). And so, by reporting the pouring out of the Spirit, first upon the disciples, and, subsequently, upon Cornelius and his household, and also by reporting Peter's statements which connect the latter gift of the Spirit to the former, Luke teaches that there is a pattern of Spirit-baptism. It is an inaugural reception of the Spirit of prophecy attested to by the sign of speaking in tongues.

Luke teaches by reporting the teaching of Jesus as well as by reporting precedents and patterns and proof from prophecy. For example, when Jesus taught his disciples about praying he taught them that the Father would give the Holy Spirit to those who ask him (Lk. 11.13). In other words, Jesus taught the disciples to pray to receive the Holy Spirit. That the disciples understood Jesus' teaching in this way is evidenced by the prayer of Peter and John that believers in Samaria might receive the Holy Spirit (Acts 8.15-17). Jesus, moreover, identified this promised gift of the Holy Spirit as the disciples being 'baptized with the Holy Spirit' (Acts 1.4-5). Furthermore, Jesus identified the purpose for the Holy Spirit coming upon the disciples. It was so that they would receive 'power' for a worldwide witness (Acts 1.8). And so, Luke taught his audience about the Holy Spirit by recording the teaching of Jesus about the Holy Spirit.

Luke not only teaches by reporting the teaching of Jesus, but he also teaches by reporting the sermons and teaching of the apostles. For example, in Acts 2 Luke reports the signs of the pouring out of the Holy Spirit on the day of Pentecost (Acts 2.2-4), the wonder of the crowd that witnessed this miracle (Acts 2.5-13) and Peter's sermon (Acts 2.14-21). In his sermon, and his application of it to his audience (Acts 2.37-41), Peter makes six primary points about the gift of the Holy Spirit: (1) this pouring out of the Spirit is the eschatological gift of the Spirit (Acts 2.17a); (2) it is (potentially) universal—crossing all age, gender and socio-economic boundaries (Acts 2.17b-18a); (3) it is the pouring out of the Spirit of prophecy (Acts 2.17b-18); (4) tongues-speaking is the sign of the pouring out of the Spirit of prophecy (Acts 2.19, cf. Acts 2.4); (5) this gift of the Spirit is the promised Spirit-baptism (Acts 2.33, cf. 1.4, 5); and (6) this pouring out of the Spirit of prophecy is available from generation to generation (Acts 2.38, 39). And so, Luke teaches a complex set of theological truths by reporting Peter's sermon.

Finally, Luke teaches by using established theological terms. For example, Luke's most frequent term to report the activity of the Holy Spirit is 'filled with the Holy Spirit' (πίμπλημι: Lk. 1.15, 41, 67; Acts 2.4; 4.8, 31; 9.17; 13.9; πληρόω: 13.52). This term appears in LXX five times (though there the form is ἐμπίμπλημι, rather than Luke's πίμπλημι). It appears each time in LXX in a charismatic context (Exod. 28.31; 31.3; 35.31; Deut. 34.9; and Isa. 11.1-3).[6] In Luke's two-volume historical narrative about Jesus and his disciples 'filled with the Holy Spirit' terminology appears either in a context of a prophetic ministry (Lk. 1.15-17) or of prophetic inspiration (Lk. 1.41, 67; Acts 2.4; 4.8, 31; 13.9). Not only the term 'filled with the Holy Spirit' but every term which Luke uses to report the activity of the Holy Spirit, with the single exception of the 'baptized with the Holy Spirit' terminology, is to be found in charismatic contexts in LXX. Clearly, the meaning of these terms is not derived exclusively from Luke's narrative itself, but is conditioned by the way the same term is used in LXX, the Bible of both Luke and his first readers. And so, by describing the activity of the

6.   I use the term 'charismatic' here and throughout this book with the specific and limited context of a person's Spirit-empowered ministry.

Holy Spirit in the life of Jesus, and in the lives of other men and women of God, by using Septuagintal terminology, Luke teaches that this activity is likewise invariably charismatic. These examples, which are merely the tip of a huge iceberg of potential examples, illustrate the various ways Luke uses historical narrative for didactic purposes.

The didactic dimension of Luke's multiplex purpose is complemented by a theological dimension. He identifies his subject to be 'all that Jesus began to do and teach' (Acts 1.1, cf. Lk. 1.5–24.51) and, because he continues his narrative about the acts of Jesus with a narrative about the acts of the apostles, Acts is by implication the complementary subject of what the apostles, empowered by the same Spirit as their Messiah, also did and taught. Thus, the primary subject is theological; specifically, it is primarily about Christ, salvation and the Holy Spirit. Therefore, in the same manner that Luke conceived the writing of historical narrative to be for the purpose of instruction or teaching so he also conceived the writing of historical narrative to be for the purpose of teaching theological truth. Through using this multiplex historical-didactic-theological purpose, Luke places himself in the historical tradition of the editors and chroniclers of the sacred history of Israel.

This discussion of Luke's multiplex purpose commends itself for the following reasons: (1) it escapes the charge of reductionism; (2) it does not confuse the original audience's real or imagined pastoral or apologetic use of Luke–Acts with Luke's purpose for writing his document; and (3) it does not identify the interests of subsequent interpreters with Luke's purpose.

3. *Applying Luke–Acts*

Applying the intended teaching of historical narrative (Luke–Acts) to contemporary Christian living is not simply like applying the imperatives of the Law, the lament or worship of the Psalms, the complementary theology and instruction of the epistles or the visions of the Apocalypse. Applying Luke–Acts requires its own set of guidelines. These include, but are not limited to: (1) apply the paradigm; (2) do not apply the historically particular; and (3) apply the principle but not the practice.

The study of Scripture is a twofold task: first, interpretation, and secondly, application. These two interdependent tasks are not, however, always kept in complementary balance. Interpretation without application is like cooking a meal and then not eating it; application without interpretation is like eating the ingredients of the meal without cooking them. The issue of application is one of appropriateness and relevancy and contrary to the facile applications which are all too often made is, perhaps, the most challenging and difficult dimension of the study of Scripture. Therefore, just as there must be appropriate guidelines for interpreting Luke–Acts in order for the interpreter to understand the document as Luke intended it to be understood, so there must also be appropriate guidelines for applying the message of Luke–Acts in order that the Christian might do the things which Luke intended to be applicable for generations of Christians subsequent to that generation of his immediate audience.

3.1. *Apply the Paradigm*

If one takes seriously Luke's narrative structure as a clue to his didactic intention, then it is self-evident that each episode fits into his narrative in a variety of ways. For example, Luke's two inauguration narratives (Lk. 3.1–4.30; Acts 1.12–2.41) are programmatic for the subsequent ministries of Jesus and then of his disciples and their converts. Luke's reports about confirmatory miracles and the complementary approval/ disapproval response theme, the travel narrative and the trials narrative illustrate, advance and extend the themes about the eschatological prophetic ministry which Luke introduced in his two inauguration narratives. There is a widespread, growing consensus among interpreters about this. There remains, however, considerable disagreement about how to apply Luke's message about the gift of the Spirit of prophecy to the contemporary Church.

There are two basic, but opposite, approaches to applying Luke's message about the gift of the Spirit of prophecy to contemporary Christian living. One approach, characteristic of many, though not all, non-Pentecostals, insists that because Luke wrote historical narrative, Luke–Acts has little to say to contemporary experience. John R.W. Stott, for example, writes:

> The revelation of the purpose of God in Scripture should be sought in its *didactic*, rather than in its *historical* parts. More precisely, we should look for it in the teachings of Jesus, and in the sermons and writings of the apostles rather than in the purely narrative portions of the Acts.[7]

7.   John R.W. Stott, *Baptism and Fullness* (London: Inter-Varsity Press, 1975), pp. 8-9 (his italics). In response to my criticism of what he wrote here, Stott has clarified and qualified his position in his recent commentary, *The Spirit, the Church,*

Similarly, Gordon Fee asserts that

> unless Scripture explicitly tells us we must do something, what is merely narrated or described can never function in a normative way.[8]

Interpreters, such as Stott and Fee, who write about the 'purely narrative portions of the Acts', or who write about what Luke has 'merely narrated' have, I believe, a non-Lukan perspective on historical narrative. They both advocate and themselves practice a hermeneutic of denial. In the light of Luke's narrative strategy, and his clear multiplex historical-didactic-theological purpose, there are no 'purely narrative portions' and, further, Luke has never 'merely narrated' anything.

In contrast to the advocates of this hermeneutic of denial many interpreters, mainly Pentecostals and charismatics, advocate a hermeneutic of affirmation. Though it may be expressed in a variety of ways, both academic and popular, the advocates of the hermeneutic of affirmation affirms that Jesus' inaugural reception of the Spirit of prophecy is a paradigm for the disciples' reception of the Spirit of prophecy. In addition, they affirm that the disciples' inaugural reception of the Spirit of prophecy is a paradigm for new converts, such as Cornelius and his household (Acts 10.44-48), and the disciples at Ephesus (Acts 19.1-7) also to receive the Spirit of prophecy.[9] These affirmations are based

---

and the World (Downers Grove, IL: InterVarsity Press, 1990). He writes: 'I am not denying that historical narratives have a didactic purpose, for of course Luke was both a historian and a theologian; I am rather affirming that a narrative's didactic purpose is not always apparent within itself and so often needs interpretive help from elsewhere in Scripture' (p. 8). This statement represents a significant shift from what he wrote in his earlier work, *Baptism and Fullness*. Nevertheless, until Stott actually states how historical narrative functions in a didactic and theological way he has not really set aside the impression that he had left with his readers; namely, that historical narrative does not communicate the purpose of God for later readers of Scripture.

8. In Fee and Stuart, *How to Read the Bible*, p. 97.

9. Contra Fee, 'Hermeneutics', p. 129. According to Fee the analogies of both Jesus' reception of the Spirit and subsequently that of the disciples is 'ruled out as irrelevant' for twentieth-century Christian experience. Such a conclusion is purely gratuitous, having no basis in the exegesis of any text of Luke–Acts. If even Old Testament examples can be relevant for the experience of Christians (e.g. Rom. 4.23; 15.4; 1 Cor. 10.6, etc.) then Fee's position on the reception of the Spirit by Jesus and the disciples is an indefensible negation. In adopting his position Fee has missed the obvious Lukan perspective; namely, that the Messianic age, which is also the era of the Spirit, began with the birth announcements of John and Jesus.

upon the observations that Peter identifies the gift of the Spirit to Cornelius to be the same as the earlier pouring out of the Spirit of prophecy on the day of Pentecost (Acts 11.15-17), and that Luke reports about the disciples at Ephesus receiving the Spirit in language which echoes and actually summarizes his description of the pouring out of the Spirit of prophecy on the day of Pentecost—'they [began] speaking with tongues [cf. Acts 2.4] and prophesying [cf. Acts 2.17, 18]'. Those interpreters who both advocate and practice this hermeneutic of affirmation also affirm that Luke intends this paradigm about the pouring out of the Spirit of prophecy to extend to all believers, for he has reported Peter to announce: 'For the promise [that you shall receive the gift of the Holy Spirit] is for you and your children, and for all who are far off' (Acts 2.39).

Each interpreter of Luke–Acts must, therefore, decide whether the hermeneutic of denial or whether the hermeneutic of affirmation best reflects Luke's narratival intentionality.

3.2. *Do Not Apply the Historically Particular*
Closely related to the issue of narrative structure and strategy on the problem of the applicability of historical narrative is the question of historical particularity. The stories of Jesus and the disciples are historically particular even when they have a programmatic/paradigmatic function. For example, both Jesus and the disciples are anointed/baptized with the Holy Spirit to inaugurate their ministries. Jesus, however, is at the Jordan when he is anointed by the Spirit; whereas the disciples are in Jerusalem when they are baptized by the Spirit. Further, the voice from heaven and the descent of the Spirit in bodily form like a dove are the auditory and ocular signs which attest to Jesus' anointing; whereas, the sound of a violent wind from heaven and the tongues of fire are the auditory and ocular signs which attest to the disciples' Spirit-baptism. These differences of historical particularity do not mean that Jesus' inaugural reception of the Spirit differs in function from the disciples' inaugural reception of the Spirit.

What is true for the gift of the Holy Spirit first to Jesus (Luke 3–4), and subsequently to the disciples (Acts 1–2), is similarly true for subsequent gifts of the Spirit reported in Acts. Thus, the occasions of the gift of the Spirit to the believers at Samaria (Acts 8), the household of

Thus, Pentecost is not the 'great line of demarcation' which Fee arbitrarily asserts it to be.

Cornelius, the Roman centurion (Acts 10), or to the disciples at Ephesus (Acts 19) are reported according to the historical particularity of each event, rather than according to some theological formula. For example, the gift of the Spirit to the believers at Samaria follows their baptism by a significant time lapse and is administered by the laying on of hands; whereas the gift of the Spirit to Cornelius and his household is on the same day as their conversion and is the sign which justifies their baptism in water, and the gift of the Spirit to the disciples at Ephesus follows their rebaptism and is administered by the laying on of hands. These episodes contrast with the gift of the Spirit to the disciples on the day of Pentecost (which was not administered by the laying on of hands). They had only received John's baptism, and were disciples of up to three years' standing. Nevertheless, each subsequent episode, despite the differences of historical particularity, illustrates the extension of the same gift of the Spirit to Samaritans, Gentiles and John's disciples as had been received by the disciples on the day of Pentecost. This conclusion is not debatable, for Peter explicitly identifies the experience of Cornelius and his household with that of the disciples on the day of Pentecost (Acts 11.17). Therefore, just as the gift signified charismatic empowering for Jesus and for the disciples on the day of Pentecost so it must also signify charismatic empowering not only for Cornelius and his household, but also for the earlier gift of the Spirit to the believers at Samaria and the later gift of the Spirit to the disciples at Ephesus.

From the above, it is clear that the historical particularity associated with these five receptions of the Holy Spirit defies all attempts at reducing the gift of the Spirit to some theological formula involving: (1) the matter of prayer; (2) the relationship to John's baptism; (3) the chronological gap between belief and reception of the Spirit; (4) the administration of the gift by the laying on of hands. None of these factors is, therefore, to be applied to the contemporary reception of the Spirit. Rather, these episodes simply show that wherever the gospel spreads, God's people can and should receive the charismatic empowering of the Spirit for their Christian service. This gift of the Spirit for charismatic empowering may be received as an individual experience or as part of a group experience; it may be in the context of prayer or it may not; it may be administered by the laying on of hands or apart from any human agency; it may be nearly simultaneous with conversion or it may be later; and finally, it may precede water baptism or follow it. Clearly, the contemporary reception of the charismatic empowering of the Spirit will have its own contemporary particularity just as it had historical particularity for the early Christian community.

3.3. *Apply the Principle but Not the Practice*

The need to distinguish between the praxis, that is, the practices, of the early Church which are reported in Acts and principle, is a particular instance of the necessity of recognizing the historical particularity of each episode in Luke's narrative. This is especially important for the question of whether or not early Church praxis can be applied to the contemporary Church and, if so, how it is to be properly applied.

In Acts, Luke reports many practices or customs among the early Christians. This is not surprising because Christianity arose out of Judaism with its legacy of religious customs. As Christianity separated from Judaism and established its own identity, it, nevertheless, retained many of the essential features of the religious praxis of Judaism. Because they knew Jesus to be the once-for-all sacrifice for sins, the disciples dropped the sacrificial dimension of worship. However, they continued to perpetuate practices or customs such as set hours of prayer, regular assembly for worship, baptism of converts, common meals, and so on. These were recognized to be compatible with the expression of their new life in the messianic age, and, like the transformation of the Passover meal into the Lord's Supper, were transformed and adapted to the new Christian reality. As reported in Acts, the practices of the early Church included: (1) establishing appropriate leadership for the community; (2) water baptism; (3) common meals; (4) regular meetings; (5) the laying on of hands; (6) prophecy as enacted parable; and, as some interpreters would add, (7) speaking in tongues.

The practice of the faith in the contemporary Church relates to this early Church practice in two ways. On the one hand, some practices are to be perpetuated in the contemporary Church; that is, they are applicable transculturally and transtemporally. Specifically, these are the Lord's Supper and water baptism. They are to be practiced by the contemporary Church because they are established by the Lord. The mode or manner for the practice of the Lord's Supper and water baptism may, however, vary in time and place. Evangelicals concede this *de facto* for the Lord's Supper, which they do not celebrate as a common meal. Those in the Anabaptist or Believer's Church tradition are more reluctant to concede this for the mode of water baptism. Clearly, however, the essential thing is the meaning of the praxis rather than the mode.

On the other hand, many early Church practices are not commanded by the Lord, and their continued practice in the contemporary Church is as much a matter of indifference as is the mode by which they may be practiced. These include such things as set times for prayer, customary times for assembly, the method(s) of establishing leadership, among orders. In other words, the contemporary Church need not pray at the ninth hour (Acts 3.1), or choose its leaders by the drawing of lots (Acts 1.21), or establish leadership in units of twelve (Acts 1.16-26), or in units of seven (Acts 6.3), or hold property in common (Acts 2.44; 4.32-37). These are matters of the historical particularity of the early Church and the contemporary Church is under no biblical/hermeneutical compulsion to apply any of this early Church praxis to its own situation.

Though the contemporary Church is under no obligation to perpetuate these practices, the practices contain principles which are obligatory for contemporary Christians. For example, Acts does not oblige Christians to pray at a customary or set time, such as 3 pm, but it teaches the principle that Christians ought to pray regularly. Similarly, though Acts does not oblige Christians to choose leadership by any one method, such as drawing lots, it does teach the principle that the Church is to have a properly established leadership and organization. Further, though Acts does not oblige contemporary Christians to practice voluntary communism, it does teach the principle that the Church, constituted of its members individual and collectively, is to minister to the needs of its poor and/or disenfranchised members. In conclusion, on the one hand, contemporary Christians are to apply the early Church praxis of the Lord's Supper and water baptism, though the mode of the practice may be a matter of indifference; on the other hand, for the non-obligatory customs or practices which were found in the early Church contemporary Christians are to apply the principles inherent within the practice, rather than the practice itself.

Speaking in tongues, as reported by Luke, is sometimes included in the debate concerning the applicability of early Church praxis to contemporary Christian experience.[10] It, therefore, requires special comment. To include speaking in tongues within the discussion on praxis is a confusion of categories. Speaking in tongues, as reported by Luke

10. Fee and Stuart, *How to Read the Bible*, p. 88. Fee includes the 'practice' of baptism of the Holy Spirit accompanied by the speaking in tongues along with the practices such as baptism, the Lord's Supper and church polity, etc.

(Acts 2.4; 10.46; 19.6), is not a practice like establishing church government, or even like celebrating the Lord's Supper or undergoing water baptism. Speaking in tongues is an objective spiritual reality. It is a gift from God and not a human rite. Therefore, it is inappropriate to include it in a discussion about applying practices within the early Church to contemporary Christian practice, as some do, often with an implicit or explicit motivation of discrediting Pentecostal theology.

To sum up, the hermeneutical question of the applicability of historical narrative, that is, Acts, to contemporary Christian experience and praxis is found to be complex. Thus, that hermeneutical stance which reduces 'the revelation of the purpose of God in Scripture...[to] its didactic, rather than its historical parts', or which asserts 'what is merely narrated or described can never function in a normative way' is seen to be a case of special pleading, and needs to be rejected for the arbitrary principle that it is. When the interpreter, having done his or her exegesis of the narrative in Acts, addresses the challenge of applying this message of that text to contemporary Christian living, he or she will be guided by several complementary and interdependent guidelines: (1) apply the lessons of a paradigmatic narrative; (2) apply the principle inherent in a relevant episode, rather than the details of historical particularity; and (3) apply the principle inherent in a particular practice, rather than the practice itself. When applied in the light of these guidelines, the narratives of Acts will spiritually enrich contemporary Christian living. However, where Acts remains shut out of contemporary relevance by a hermeneutic which is either hostile or antipathetic to the contemporary applicability of historical narrative, spiritual impoverishment will remain.

Reading, interpreting and applying Luke–Acts in the ways discussed above—and there are also other, even more sophisticated ways—proves to be an incredibly illuminating, enriching enterprise. It opens up in new and fresh ways the message of a quarter of the New Testament. It enables the reader to discover Luke's historical-didactic-theological purposes that a more traditional hermeneutic of historical narrative suppresses. One of the great discoveries is Luke's charismatic theology, more specifically his portrait of the people of God as the prophethood of all believers.

Chapter 2

JESUS: THE PROPHET MIGHTY IN WORD AND DEED (LUKE 1–24)

In Acts Luke describes the eschatological people of God, upon whom Jesus, the eschatological anointed prophet, has poured out the Spirit of prophecy, as the prophethood of all believers. Luke's vision of the prophethood of all believers is given biblical definition and delineation in an ancient oracle of the prophet Joel which finds fulfillment beginning with the pouring out of the Holy Spirit upon the disciples on the day of Pentecost. But the new age of prophecy began about one generation earlier with the birth announcements of John the Baptist and Jesus of Nazareth and reached its ultimate expression in the brief ministry of Jesus, the uniquely anointed prophet.

The following five chapters will explore Luke's vision of the prophethood of all believers, a vision which, when properly understood, is his greatest contribution to his doctrine of the people of God. In this chapter I will survey Luke's portrait of Jesus as the anointed prophet. In the following chapter I will discuss Luke's Pentecost narrative, which reports the transfer of the Spirit of prophecy from Jesus to his disciples (Acts 2.1-41). In Chapters 4–6 I will shift the focus from the origin of the prophetic community to the acts of the prophetic community and, finally, to the acts of six individual prophets: namely, Stephen (Acts 6.8–7.60), Philip (Acts 8.1-40), Peter (Acts 9.32–12.24), Barnabas (Acts 11.19-26), Agabus (Acts 11.27-30) and Paul (Acts 12.25–28.31).

1. Jesus: The Anointed Prophet[1]

In his narrative history of the origin of Christianity Luke portrays the founder of Christianity, Jesus the son of Mary and Joseph, in language

---

1. The subject of Jesus and his disciples as prophets has recently received much scholarly attention. Important and readily available treatments include: Paul S. Minear, *To Heal and to Reveal: Prophetic Vocation According to Luke* (New

larger than life. For example, though Jesus is born into a peasant home at a time when his people are humiliated by the domination of a foreign power, he is announced to be the heir to the royal throne of his father David, Israel's illustrious king (Lk. 1.32-35). Further, at his birth angels announce that this king elect is a savior (Lk. 2.11), a title which not only gives him a status equal to Hellenistic kings such as the Ptolemies or Roman emperors such as Julius Caesar, Nero or Vespasian,[2] but which also ranks him with the God of Israel (Deut. 32.15) and as a rival to the gods of the Greco-Roman world, such as Zeus, Apollo and Hermes.[3] This one who is savior is also announced to be Christ the Lord (Lk. 2.11). The title 'Christ' identifies Jesus as the Anointed One, whereas, the title 'Lord' identifies him both with the God of Israel and as a rival to kings such as Herod the Great and to the Roman lord, or Caesar.[4] Such titles—Davidic King, Savior, Christ and Lord—when applied to a peasant baby are inappropriate and, indeed, both blasphemous and seditious, except for the transcendent fact that by virtue of his unique conception by the overshadowing power of the Spirit, he is the Son of God (Lk. 1.35).

2. Jesus: The Eschatological Prophet

Though Luke portrays Jesus as larger than life through these titles both royal and divine, he also portrays him as a man in human society. For example, Jesus begins his public ministry as a teacher, very much after the commonplace pattern of a rabbi and his disciples (Lk. 4.31–6.49). In addition, his actions quickly alert people to the fact that he is more

York: Seabury, 1976); David Hill, *New Testament Prophecy* (Atlanta: John Knox Press, 1976); David E. Aune, *Prophecy in Early Christianity and the Ancient Mediterranean World* (Grand Rapids: Eerdmans, 1983); Robert P. Menzies, *Empowered for Witness: The Spirit in Luke–Acts* (JPTSup, 6; Sheffield: Sheffield Academic Press, 1994); and Turner, *Power from on High*.

2.   James Hope Moulton and George Milligan, *The Vocabulary of the Greek New Testament Illustrated from the Papyri and Other Non-Literary Sources* (Grand Rapids: Eerdmans, 1963), p. 621.

3.   LSJ, p. 1751.

4.   Moulton and Milligan, *Vocabulary of the Greek New Testament*, p. 365. There is no evidence that the title Κύριος was applied to Augustus, who was in power when Jesus was born. However, by the time Luke had written his narrative about Jesus and the apostles it had been applied to Claudius (41–54 CE) and becomes very common in the time of Nero (54–68 CE).

than a teacher: he is recognized to be a prophet (Lk. 7.16), like one of the prophets of old (Lk. 9.19). This reputation of being a prophet, which he has earned by the character of his ministry, echoes his own self-consciousness, for he began his public ministry by identifying himself with the two charismatic prophets, Elijah and Elisha (Lk. 4.25-27).

A close reading of Luke's history of the origin of Christianity compels the reader to conclude that Jesus ministers, from first to last, as the eschatological, anointed prophet. Indeed, this portrait of Jesus as prophet is what primarily distinguishes the Jesus-according-to-Luke from the Jesus-according-to-Matthew, Mark or John. Luke informs his readers that Jesus' public ministry, from first to last, is that of the eschatological prophet by adopting the narrative strategy called inclusio. Jesus' self-identification as a prophet in the inauguration narrative (Lk. 3.1–4.44) introduces the theme, and the disciples' identification of Jesus as a prophet mighty in work and word after the resurrection (Lk. 24.19) concludes the theme in terms of his earthly ministry. The first reference is programmatic for his subsequent ministry; the second is a retrospective assessment of that ministry. Thus from the descent of the Spirit upon him at his baptism (Lk. 3.22), which he understands to be his anointing (Lk. 4.18-21), to his death, where he is crucified as the 'rejected prophet' (Lk. 23.1; 24.19-20), everything which Luke reports Jesus as doing and saying are the works and words of the eschatological, anointed prophet.

Jesus identifies himself as prophet in his inaugural sermon at Nazareth (Lk. 4.16-30). Because this is programmatic for Jesus' entire ministry, Luke has placed this episode immediately after Jesus' baptism and temptation, and thereby at the beginning of Jesus' ministry rather than later, as Mark places it.[5] Jesus identifies his own situation at Nazareth—no prophet is welcome in his home town (Lk. 4.24)—with that of Elijah, who left Israel to minister to a Gentile widow in Zarephath (Lk. 4.25-26), and that of Elisha, whom the Lord used to cleanse a Gentile leper, Naaman the Syrian (Lk. 4.27). This identification of Jesus with these prophets is itself a self-fulfilling prophecy, for Jesus will

---

5.   Whereas Luke reports Jesus' inaugural visit to the synagogue in Nazareth immediately after his baptism (Lk. 3.21-22) and his temptation (Lk. 4.1-13), Mark does not report it until much later in Jesus' ministry (Mk 6.1-6). In light of the fact that his rejection by his townspeople in Nazareth is the reason for his move to Capernaum, where Mark reports him located as early as 1.21, it is likely that Luke has preserved the correct chronology.

quickly become unwelcome in his home town (Lk. 4.28-29) and, like Elijah and Elisha, will turn from his own people to minister to others (Lk. 4.29-30).

Even before Luke's report of this, however, he has reported extensively Jesus' experience of the Spirit: Jesus was anointed by the Spirit (Lk. 3.22/4.18), full of the Spirit—a stative or durative experience (Lk. 4.1a)—led by the Spirit (Lk. 4.1b) and empowered by the Spirit (Lk. 4.14). These descriptions of Jesus' experience of the Spirit are, like the inauguration address, programmatic for Jesus' entire ministry—in other words, Luke expects that his readers will understand that, from first to last, Jesus is full of the Spirit, led by the Spirit and empowered by the Spirit.

That Jesus is a man of the Spirit from first to last, that is, a charismatic prophet, is confirmed by two of his own disciples after his crucifixion (Lk. 24.13-35). As these disciples walk to Emmaus, Jesus, crucified but risen, joins them and asks what they have been talking about (Lk. 24.17). Not recognizing him they tell him what befell Jesus the Nazarene and identify him as a 'prophet mighty in deed and word' in the sight of God and all the people (Lk. 24.19).[6] This identification of Jesus as prophet by his disciples, is retrospective of his entire ministry. Jesus has identified himself as prophet (Lk. 4.25-27) and is recognized as a prophet by others (Lk. 7.16). Further, his prophetic ministry has been recognized to be mighty, that is, powerful (δυνατός), an echo of the programmatic description of 4.14. Moreover, this prophetic power is twofold. First, he is a prophet powerful in deed (literally, in 'works'). As Luke reports it, his power characteristically extends to casting out demons (Lk. 4.31-37), healing the sick (Lk. 4.38-39) and, above all, raising the dead (Lk. 7.11-17), which is the work uniquely associated with the charismatic prophets Elijah and Elisha. Second, he is a prophet powerful in word—forgiving sins (Lk. 5.20), pronouncing blessings (Lk. 6.20-23) and dire curses (Lk. 6.25-26). This understanding of Jesus

---

6. This text supplies the title for James B. Shelton's fine monograph on Luke's theology of the Holy Spirit: *Mighty in Word and Deed: The Role of the Holy Spirit in Luke–Acts* (Peabody, MA: Hendrickson, 1991). Shelton's thesis is that, 'Luke was often pointing to the role of the Holy Spirit in effecting miracles and inspiring witness' (p. 4). My thesis is that works empowered by the Spirit and words inspired by the Spirit are the complementary components of a *prophetic* ministry, both for Jesus and the disciples. Shelton, I believe, fails to explicate fully this *prophetic* dimension of Luke's charismatic theology.

by these two disciples is echoed years later by Peter when he witnesses to the household of Cornelius about Jesus: 'how God anointed Him with the Holy Spirit and power, and, how he went about doing good, and healing all who were oppressed by the devil; for God was with him' (Acts 10.38). In addition, this retrospective assessment of Jesus' ministry is also echoed in the transitional introduction to Luke's second book: 'The first book I composed', Luke reminds Theophilus, was 'about all that Jesus began to do and teach' (Acts 1.1), that is, about his mighty works and words.

3. *The Infancy Narrative: The Restoration of Prophecy*

Luke's strategy of inclusio compels the reader to understand that Jesus' entire public ministry is that of the eschatological, anointed prophet—powerful in works and word from first to last. But Jesus' ministry as prophet was not unprecedented except in its ultimate scope. In the ongoing history of salvation it was preceded by, and arose out of, an outburst of prophetic activity associated with the birth announcements of John the Baptist and of Jesus. It is this prophetic outburst, with which the Gospel opens which, in the ongoing history of salvation, was unprecedented. It was unprecedented because, with a few exceptions (notably John Hyrcanus and a few Essene prophets),[7] prophecy had ceased in Israel.[8]

In contrast to the historically isolated and very rare reports of prophecy in the intertestamental period, the dramatic outburst of prophecy which Luke reports in his infancy narrative is, representationally, a community-wide renewal and restoration of prophecy. Joel had announced this very thing: the Spirit would be poured out upon all flesh. Specifically, Joel promised to Israel: 'your sons and daughters shall prophecy, your young men shall see visions, and your old men shall dream dreams; even upon My bondslaves, both men and women, I will pour forth of My Spirit' (Joel 2.28). Fulfilling Joel's promise that sons and daughters shall prophesy, sons, such as John who is filled with the Spirit (Lk. 1.15), and daughters such as Mary (whose song, the Magnificat [Lk. 1.48-55], must be identified as prophecy on the analogy

---

7.   Josephus, *War* 1.68-69; *Ant.* 13.311-13; 15.373-78; 17.345-48.

8.   The belief in the cessation of prophecy in Israel is explicit in the following texts: 2 *Bar.* 85.3; *Apion* 1.41; and *t. Sot.* 6.2. It is implicit in texts such as 1 Macc. 4.46; 14.44.

of the Songs of Elizabeth [Lk. 1.42-44] and Zacharias [Lk. 1.68-79]), prophesy. In addition to young men, such as John, old men, such as Zacharias (who, incidently, has a vision [Lk. 1.22]), and Simeon (who has the Spirit upon him, has had revelations by the Spirit, and who is also led by the Spirit [Lk. 2.25-27]), prophesy (Lk. 1.67-79; 2.28-32). Further, bondslaves, both men, such as Simeon (Lk. 2.29), and women, such as Mary (Lk. 1.38), fulfill Joel's announcement. Finally, Luke also reports about the aged prophetess, Anna (Lk. 2.36-38). And so, in the outpouring of the Spirit in the infancy narrative John, Elizabeth, Mary, Zacharias, Simeon and Anna represent a prophetic community. Young and old, male and female, and even bondslaves prophesy when the Spirit is poured out in Israel once again. Thus, Luke's infancy narrative reports the restoration of prophecy among God's people.

According to the theology of Judaism the coming of the Messiah and the pouring out of the Spirit, that is, the renewal and restoration of prophecy, are complementary events. Luke's infancy narrative corresponds to this perspective, for this unprecedented outburst of prophecy is, without exception, clustered around the birth of the one who is not only Israel's Savior, but who is also 'Christ the Lord' (Lk. 2.11). In other words, he is the Messiah. Thus, the complementary outburst of prophecy and the birth of Jesus herald the dawning of the last days. The new, messianic age has arrived. This transition from the former days to the last days, which Luke reports in his infancy narrative, means that this outburst of prophecy is the eschatological gift of prophecy.

Not only does this restoration of prophecy, which Luke reports, herald the coming of the Messiah and, therefore, the turning point in history, but it is also the precursor to the eschatological prophetic community that the Messiah, himself the eschatological prophet, will subsequently establish to be the heir and successor to his prophetic ministry. The community dimension of the restoration of prophecy which is found in the individual representatives such as John, Elizabeth, Mary, Zacharias, Simeon and Anna, becomes actualized in the experience of the 120 disciples who all prophesy when Jesus pours out the Spirit upon them on the day of Pentecost (Acts 2.1-21).

4. *The Prophetic Ministry of Jesus*

Between this representative prophetic community of the infancy narrative (Lk. 1.5–2.52) and the actualization of the prophetic community, beginning with the Pentecost narrative (Acts 2.1-41), stands the public ministry of Jesus, the eschatological, anointed prophet. Luke portrays the prophetic ministry of Jesus using a variety of prophetic themes, motifs, types and actions, both implicit and explicit. Luke marshals a massive quantity of data to complete his portrait of Jesus as prophet. Indeed, the interpreter of Luke's narrative finds a surfeit rather than a scarcity of data to discuss. In what follows I will limit my discussion to five themes concerning Jesus as prophet. According to Luke, throughout his ministry Jesus is variously: (1) a prophet like Isaiah; (2) a charismatic prophet like Elijah and Elisha; (3) the rejected prophet; (4) the prophet like Moses; and (5) the royal prophet.

Before discussing these five prophetic themes in Luke's narrative about Jesus, I will first lay the foundation for Luke's portrait of Jesus as prophet by surveying his data about Jesus' identification as a prophet. Jesus' experience of the Spirit begins in that grand miracle which the angel Gabriel announced to Mary about the son whom she is about to conceive in her womb (Lk. 1.26-34): 'The Holy Spirit will come upon you, and the power of the Most High will overshadow you; and for that reason the holy offspring shall be called the Son of God' (Lk. 1.35). This promise establishes the absolute and eternal uniqueness of Jesus ontologically—he is truly God and truly human. About a generation later Jesus begins a new relationship with the Spirit. At his baptism, Luke reports, 'the Holy Spirit descended upon him in bodily form like a dove' (Lk. 3.22a). Thus Jesus was anointed by the Holy Spirit for ministry (Lk. 4.18; Acts 10.38).

Excursus: Royal Son or Anointed Prophet?
After the Holy Spirit had descended upon Jesus, '...a voice came out of heaven, "Thou art My beloved Son, in Thee I am well-pleased"' (Lk. 3.22b). 'Heaven' is a reverential circumlocution for God. Therefore, complementing the descent of the Spirit upon Jesus, God addressed words of sonship and approval to him in the language of the psalms (Ps. 2.7) and the Prophets (Isa. 42.1). Theophilus, and every reader of Luke's narrative, advancing from the Inauguration Narrative (Lk. 3–4), would naturally interpret this address at Jesus' baptismal experience to identify him as the Davidic, royal son or Messiah.

Once David became established on the throne he became Israel's dynastic head, and his son and subsequent kings in Judah came to the throne on the basis of heredity. Luke's infancy narrative, therefore, establishes Jesus to be the legitimate hereditary heir to David's now vacant throne. Mary, to whom Jesus will be born, is engaged to Joseph, 'of the descendants of David' (Lk. 1.27). Concerning her son the angel Gabriel announces: 'the Lord God will give Him the throne of His father David' (Lk. 1.32b). Further, because he is of the house and family of David, when Caesar Augustus orders the census Joseph takes Mary with him from Nazareth, 'to Judea, the city of David' (i.e. Bethlehem, Lk. 2.4). Finally, when Jesus is born to Mary and Joseph in Bethlehem, an angel announces to some shepherds: 'today in the city of David there has been born for you a Savior, who is Christ the Lord' (Lk. 2.11). Though all three terms—'Savior', 'Christ' and 'Lord'— have a variety of meanings in various appropriate contexts, here in the context of Jesus' birth as a descendant of David the terms 'Savior', 'Christ' and 'Lord' are royal titles.

Kingship within David's dynasty is hereditary. But as the example of David's son, Solomon, reminds us, kingship was a matter of divine choice, and was also established by the act of anointing (1 Kgs 1.1-40). Therefore, Jesus' Jordan experience necessarily complements his birth as David's heir to the throne. In other words, the one who was born king in Bethlehem is necessarily anointed king at the Jordan.

Though he is born the royal heir in Bethlehem and is anointed to kingship at the Jordan, Jesus' subsequent ministry in and around Galilee is *not* that of a royal son. This is indicated by several lines of evidence. On the one hand, Jesus is never in Jerusalem, the royal city, during his public ministry (Lk. 4–18). On the other hand, the title 'Lord', as a royal title, is never applied to Jesus until, for the first time, according to Luke's narrative, he arrives at Jericho when en route to Jerusalem (Lk. 18.35-43). At Jericho a blind beggar addresses Jesus as 'Son of David' (Lk. 18.38, 39), language which has not been applied to Jesus since Luke 1–2. Further, while still at Jericho Jesus told the parable of the absent nobleman who went to a distant country to receive a kingdom for himself, 'because he was near Jerusalem, and they supposed that the kingdom of God was going to appear immediately' (Lk. 19.11, 12). As Jesus approached Jerusalem the multitude of disciples acclaimed him as their king: 'Blessed is the king who comes in the name of the Lord' (Lk. 19.38). In spite of this enthusiastic acclaim the Jewish nation will reject him as their king, and the Romans will execute him under the mocking superscription 'This is the King of the Jews' (Lk. 23.38). But God vindicates this rejected and murdered king by raising him from the dead. This vindication is consummated in

Jesus' ascension and exaltation, that is, his enthronement at the right hand of God (Acts 2.33-35), when God makes him, both 'Lord and Christ' (Acts 2.36, compare Lk. 2.11).

This evidence is conclusive. Jesus is described in royal language only in Luke 1–2 and Luke 18–Acts 2. His public ministry (Lk. 4–18) is that of the anointed prophet rather than that of David's heir. How, then, is the reader to understand the address from God to Jesus at the Jordan: 'Thou art My beloved Son, in Thee I am well-pleased' (Lk. 3.22)? The quotation from Ps. 2.7 is retrospective. It looks back to the promises and announcements in the infancy narrative that a son of David will once again sit on David's throne. It confirms that Jesus of Nazareth, who has just been baptized by John, is this promised son of David. But the voice from heaven immediately proceeds to identify the nature of Jesus' public ministry. The quotation from Isa. 42.1 is prospective. It introduces the public ministry of Jesus, not as royal son but as anointed prophet. This, indeed, is Jesus' own understanding of his baptismal experience. He interprets it in the light of Isa. 61.1 (Lk. 4.25-27). Recognizing but rejecting his claim to be the anointed prophet, his own townspeople immediately attempt to kill him as a false prophet (Lk. 4.30).

To sum up, the man born to be king (Luke 1–2) is anointed king at the Jordan (Lk. 3.22), but is not enthroned as king until the ascension (Acts 2.33-36). The voice from heaven—specifically the quotation of Isa. 42.1—turns the reader away from royal sonship to a new, radically different understanding of Jesus' ministry, specifically, that for the period from the Jordan (Lk. 3) to his approach to Jerusalem (Lk. 18) Jesus ministers exclusively, and from first to last, as the anointed prophet.

Having been anointed by the Spirit, Jesus becomes the unique bearer of the Spirit and experiences the fulness of the Spirit (Lk. 4.1a), the leading (Lk. 4.1b), the empowering (Lk. 4.14), the joy (Lk. 10.21) and the inspiration of the Spirit (Acts 1.2). He teaches about the Spirit (Lk. 11.13; 12.10; 21.15) and promises the Spirit to his disciples (Lk. 12.11-12; Acts 1.4-5, 8). His incarnational experience of the Spirit ends when, after his ascension–enthronement (Acts 2.33-36), he pours forth the Spirit upon the disciples on the day of Pentecost (Acts 2.33). Thus, the Spirit is transferred from the unique bearer of the Spirit to his disciples for their ministry as his heirs and successors.

The data discussed above suggest that Luke's portrait of Jesus as king reflects David's own experience. Samuel anoints David to be king (1 Sam. 16.1-13) but, in fact, he does not become king until many years later (2 Sam. 2.1-4a). Between his earlier anointing for kingship and his becoming king over Judah at Hebron David neither functions as king, nor claims to be king, nor is identified or acknowledged as king by others. Thus, for many years David's experience is 'anointed-but-not-yet-king'. It is the same for Jesus. His anointing to be king and his enthronement approximately three years later is not the 'now-and-not-yet' of the coming of the kingdom of God. Rather it is the 'anointed-but-not-yet-king' of David's own experience.

Apart from Jesus' first experience of the Spirit, that is, his conception by the overshadowing power of the Spirit, his remaining experiences of the Spirit are all complementary to his identity as a prophet in Luke's narrative. In his inaugural synagogue homily at Nazareth Jesus identifies himself as a prophet (Lk. 4.25-27). He is identified as a prophet by others because of his works (Lk. 7.16), develops the reputation for being a prophet (Lk. 7.39; 9.7-8, 19), and is identified as a prophet by his disciples (Lk. 24.19). Though all of the evangelists identify Jesus as a prophet (e.g. Mt. 21.11, Mk 6.15 and Jn 6.14), neither individually nor collectively do they match the comprehensive and complex identification of Jesus as prophet to be found in the history of Jesus written by Luke.

4.1. *Jesus: The Isaianic Prophet*

In the order of the appearance of the five major prophetic motifs in Luke's narrative the first is Jesus as the Isaianic prophet. This theme begins at the baptism of Jesus, and it appears both visually and audibly. While Jesus was praying, '[H]eaven was opened', Luke reports, 'and the Holy Spirit descended in bodily form like a dove, and a voice came out of heaven, "Thou are My beloved Son, in thee I am well-pleased" '. The heavenly commendation of Jesus as a well-pleasing Son is the auditory echo of the servant Song (Isa. 42.1b). The visual echo of the same servant song is the descent of the Spirit, making concrete the affirmation: 'I have put My Spirit upon Him' (Isa. 42.1c). Thus, the opening words of the first Servant Song unite the seemingly independent visual and auditory phenomena of Jesus' baptismal experience. Further, this baptism experience, with its visual and auditory fulfillment of God's promise to the servant-prophet ultimately lies behind Peter's servant Christology in Acts (3.12-26).

Jesus' inaugural sermon at Nazareth continues the theme of Jesus as the Isaianic prophet. Coming to the synagogue one sabbath after his baptismal reception of the Spirit he takes part in the service, reading from Isaiah:

> The Spirit of the LORD is upon me,
> Because he anointed me to preach the gospel to the poor.
> He has sent me to proclaim release to the captives,
> And recovery of sight to the blind,
> To set free those who are downtrodden,
> To proclaim the favorable year of the LORD (Lk. 4.18, 19).

Reflecting his self-consciousness brought forward from his baptismal experience he then announces: 'Today this Scripture has been fulfilled in your hearing' (Lk. 4.21). This text from Isaiah (Isa. 61.1), in the first place, explains the significance of the descent of the Spirit upon him. It is his anointing. He is the anointed, prophetic Messiah. Thus, Peter can report years later, 'how God anointed Him [Jesus] with the Holy Spirit and with power' (Acts 10.38). This text, in the second place, establishes the program or agenda for his mission as anointed prophet. This agenda is not merely metaphorical. When two disciples of John the Baptist ask Jesus on his behalf 'Are You the One who is coming?', Luke reports, 'At that very time He cured many people of diseases and evil spirits, and He granted sight to many who were blind' (Lk. 7.20b, 21). Jesus then instructs John's disciples: 'Go and report to John what you have seen and heard: the blind receive sight, the lame walk, the lepers are cleansed, the deaf hear, the dead are raised up, the poor have the gospel preached to them' (Lk. 7.22). Since Jesus' answer to John's question explicitly echoes his Nazareth text (Isa. 61.1), and since it is not metaphorical at this point there can be little doubt that its meaning is not merely metaphorical in the Nazareth synagogue context. Indeed, subsequent to Jesus' synagogue sermon Luke variously reports that the good news of God's favorable intervention is for the poor, upon whom Jesus announces the blessing of the Kingdom of God (Lk. 6.20). The good news is, further, that captives in bonds, such as the demoniac in the country of the Gerasenes (Lk. 8.26-39), will be set free. Finally, the blind, such as the blind beggar at Jericho (Lk. 18.35-43), will receive sight. Indeed, as the anointed prophet Jesus will not only minister to the poor, the captives and the blind, but to all those who are downtrodden, the disenfranchised, such as the widow or the Samaritan, and all others who are downtrodden in sin, sickness and poverty.

Though this agenda is not merely metaphorical neither is it primarily about the Spirit of prophecy as preaching (as opposed to miracle working).[9] The replacement of the clause 'to bind up the brokenhearted' (Isa. 61.1c) by the phrase 'and recovery of sight to the blind' (Isa. 58.6) shows that Jesus has miracle-working power in his mind as much as preaching. It must be observed, further, that the words 'preach' and 'proclaim' from the Isaiah text are, in the context of Jesus' ministry, not about preaching as distinct from miracle working, for more often than not throughout his ministry he verbally 'proclaims' a miracle, that is, he effects the miracle through his spoken word. For example, Jesus 'rebuked' the fever in Simon's mother-in-law and it left her (Lk. 4.38, 39). Jesus' reply to John's question is also relevant here. The proof that he is the one whom John announced is that, in the language of Isa. 61.1, he is the (anointed) prophet (Lk. 7.16) powerful in works (e.g. the blind receive sight) and word (the poor have the gospel preached to them (Lk. 7.22).

The theme of Jesus as the Isaianic prophet is developed further in Jesus' parabolic teaching. In common with many of his prophetic predecessors, such as Ezekiel or Isaiah, Jesus typically taught in parables. Jesus did this in conscious and explicit fulfillment of Isaiah's own commissioning:

> Go and tell this people:
> Keep on listening, but do not perceive;
> Keep on looking, but do not understand (Isa. 6.9).

On one occasion when the disciples questioned Jesus about one of his parables he said to them: 'To you it is granted to know the mysteries of the Kingdom of God, but to the rest it is in parables; in order that seeing they may not see, and hearing they may not understand' (Lk. 8.10).

In summary, Isaiah supplies several themes relating to Jesus as prophet, initially focusing on the inauguration of his ministry—the heavenly voice of approval, the descent of the Spirit, which is his anointing, and subsequently focusing on other dimensions of his ministry, his role as servant, his ministry of the good news of God's favor, and his use of parables.

---

9.   Menzies, *Empowered for Witness*, pp. 145-56.

4.2. *Jesus: The Prophet Like Elijah and Elisha*

Jesus is not only the anointed Isaianic servant-prophet, he is also a prophet like Elijah and Elisha, two notable charismatic prophets of Old Testament times. This motif is introduced in the first of the two texts that form Luke's narrative strategy of inclusio for Jesus as prophet (Lk. 4.25-27). In the aftermath to his inaugural sermon in the synagogue at Nazareth Jesus challenges his fellow townspeople to honor him as the anointed (prophet) he has just identified himself to be (Lk. 4.22). He then cites the historical precedent of Elijah and Elisha, who ministered to strangers, as a warning that if they reject him as prophet he, like those former prophets, will go and minister to others (Lk. 4.25-27). Thus, Jesus begins his public ministry with the explicit consciousness that there is an affinity between these two charismatic prophets and himself.

Luke portrays Jesus' ministry as prophet, from first to last, to be charismatic. He introduces it with the programmatic summary that after his temptation: 'Jesus returned to Galilee in the power of the Spirit' (Lk. 4.14a). Early in his narrative he repeatedly returns to this theme. Thus, he introduces the healing of the paralytic with the statement: 'and the power of the Lord was present for him to perform healing' (Lk. 5.17). Later he reports: 'And all the multitude were trying to touch Him, for power was coming from Him and healing them all' (Lk. 6.19). As an example of this, when the sick woman touched him in faith, healing power went out of him (Lk. 8.46). Consistently, with this picture, after his death some of his disciples testified about him as a prophet: 'mighty [i.e. powerful, δυνατὸς] in works' (Lk. 24.19).

Jesus modeled this charismatic, Spirit-empowered prophetic ministry after the pattern of the charismatic ministries of Elijah and Elisha. For example, like Elisha who cleansed the leper, Naaman the Syrian (Lk. 4.27; 2 Kgs 5.8-14), Jesus will also cleanse lepers (Lk. 5.12). Moreover, just as Elijah and Elisha controlled nature by the miraculous manipulation of water (1 Kgs 17.1; 2 Kgs 2.8, 14, 19-22) so Jesus also controls nature, commanding even the wind and water to obey him (Lk. 8.22-25). Furthermore, just as Elijah and Elisha multiplied a little food into much food (1 Kgs 17.16; 2 Kgs 4.3-7, 42-44), so Jesus multiplies five loaves and two fish into enough food to feed a multitude numbering about 5000 men (Lk. 9.10-17). Most characteristic of all, just as Elijah and Elisha raised the dead (1 Kgs 17.17-24; 2 Kgs 4.34-39), so Jesus also raises the dead (Lk. 7.11-17; 9.49-56). Of all the powerful works which Jesus performed it is the raising of the dead which causes the people to say about him: 'A great prophet has arisen among us!' (Lk. 7.16). Inevitably it is after this miracle that Jesus has the reputation that he is either John the Baptist or Elijah or one of the other prophets of old (Lk. 9.7-8, 19).

Jesus fulfills the Elijah and Elisha pattern in one further respect. Just as the Spirit, which had empowered Elijah, was transferred from him to his disciple, Elisha, when he ascended to heaven (2 Kgs 2.9, 14-15), so the Spirit was similarly transferred to the disciples after Jesus ascended to heaven (Acts 1.9-11). Further, just as Elisha as heir and successor to Elijah performed the same kind of miracles that Elijah had earlier performed, so in Acts the disciples, as heirs and successors to Jesus' prophet ministry, will perform the same kinds of miracles that Jesus had earlier performed—healing the sick, casting out demons and even raising the dead. In other words, just as Jesus is a charismatic prophet like Elijah and Elisha, so the disciples, because they have the same empowering of the Spirit as Jesus did, and because they do the same kind of miracles as Jesus did, are a company of charismatic prophets also like Elijah and Elisha.

4.3. *Jesus: The Rejected Prophet*

The theme of the despised and rejected prophet is typical of the Old Testament historical literature. It appears there in contexts which justify God's ultimate judgment—exile—upon his people. For example, concerning the capture of Samaria and the exile of Israel to Assyria the narrative explains: 'Yet the Lord warned Israel and Judah through all His prophets and every seer... However, they did not listen, but stiffened their neck, like their fathers' (2 Kgs 17.13, 14). Similarly, concerning the capture of Jerusalem, the destruction of the temple and the exile of Judah to Babylon the narrative explains: 'And the Lord, the God of their fathers, sent [word] to them again by His messengers...but they continually mocked the messengers of God, despised His words and scoffed at His prophets' (2 Chron. 36.15, 16). From the attempt to kill Jesus in Nazareth through to his execution in Jerusalem, Jesus' experience of rejection is in the centuries-long pattern of how both Israel and Judah treated the prophets whom God sent to them.

As we have observed, Jesus has first identified himself as the Isaianic anointed prophet (Lk. 4.18-20), and then as the prophet like Elijah and Elisha (Lk. 4.24-27). He next identified himself as the rejected prophet.

Like the first two themes the rejected prophet motif is introduced in Jesus' Nazareth address (Lk. 4.16-30). Here, at the beginning of his ministry, he identifies himself as a rejected prophet after the pattern of Elijah and Elisha, who were rejected in Israel and subsequently ministered to Gentiles (Lk. 4.24-27). Enraged by Jesus' claim to be a prophet his townspeople attempt to kill him—the punishment reserved for a false prophet (Deut. 18.20)—by throwing him over a cliff (Lk. 4.28-30). From the beginning, then, in Luke's record Jesus, the divinely approved and anointed prophet (Lk. 3.22), is under the cloud of imminent rejection and death.

Jesus carries the certainty of his ultimate rejection and death with him throughout his ministry. For example, in the context where Peter reports about Jesus' reputation as a prophet like John the Baptist, Elijah or one of the other prophets (Lk. 9.19) Jesus immediately announces his death for the first time, saying: 'The Son of Man must suffer many things, and be rejected by the elders and chief priests and scribes, and be killed, and be raised on the third day' (Lk. 9.22). Moreover, Jesus indicts his future murderers as those who 'build the tombs of the prophets, and it was your fathers who killed them' (Lk. 11.48). Consequently, the generation of Jesus' day would kill some of the prophets and apostles whom God is sending to them, 'in order that the blood of all the prophets...may be charged against this generation' (Lk. 11.50). Later, when some Pharisees warn Jesus that Herod wants to kill him he solemnly affirms:

> I must journey on today and tomorrow and the next [day]; for it cannot be that a prophet should perish outside of Jerusalem. O Jerusalem, Jerusalem, [the city] that kills the prophets and stones those sent to her! (Lk. 13.33, 34a).

And so in conscious fulfillment of the rejected prophet theme Jesus journeys to Jerusalem. There he is arrested, and when he has been brought to the house of the High Priest he is mocked as prophet. As Luke reports it, 'they blindfolded Him and were asking Him, saying, "Prophesy, who is the one who hit You?"' (Lk. 22.64). Clearly, from the time of his inaugural sermon at Nazareth onwards Jesus is conscious that he will die in Jerusalem as a prophet who is rejected by his own people, just as the prophets of old were rejected and killed by Israel. Thus, as Luke emphasizes it, Jesus dies, not merely as the rejected King of the Jews (Lk. 19.11-27; 21.1-3, 36-38), but as the rejected anointed prophet. The tragedy in this is that though he 'was a prophet mighty in deed and word in the sight of God and all the people' (Lk. 24.19), the chief priests and rulers, nevertheless 'delivered Him up to the sentence of death, and crucified Him' (Lk. 24.20).

4.4. *Jesus: The Prophet Like Moses*

Jesus is also the prophet like Moses. Moses foretold this prophet, saying: 'The Lord your God will raise up for you a prophet like me from among you, from your countrymen, you shall listen to him' (Deut. 18.15). Moses' command, 'you shall listen you him', is echoed in the transfiguration account, where, not coincidently, Moses and Elijah appear with Jesus. In response to what he has just witnessed Peter proposes that they should build three tabernacles, one each for Moses, Elijah and Jesus (Lk. 9.33). At this point a voice comes out of the cloud, saying, 'This is my Son, my chosen one; listen to Him!' (Lk. 9.35). Very likely it is Peter's experience here on the so-called Mount of Transfiguration which later causes him to identify Jesus as the prophet like Moses (Acts 3.22). This apparently became a widespread identification in the early Church, for even the Hellenistic Jew, Stephen, hints at Jesus as the prophet like Moses (Acts 7.39).

The explicit 'listen to him' identification of Jesus as the prophet like Moses complements the actual transfiguration of Jesus, in which 'his appearance became different, and his clothing became white and gleaming' (Lk. 9.29). Jesus' metamorphosis here echoes Moses' earlier experience on Mt Sinai when 'the skin on his face shone because of his speaking with Him' (i.e. the Lord, Exod. 34.29). Further, when Moses and Elijah came to Jesus on the mountain, Luke reports, '[they] were speaking of his departure [literally, exodus] which He was about to accomplish in Jerusalem' (Lk. 9.31). Luke then reports that after Jesus descended from the mountain, 'he resolutely set His face to go to Jerusalem' (Lk. 9.51). The long travel narrative from Galilee to Jerusalem which follows (Lk. 9–19) contains many Moses and Exodus themes, beginning with the ministry of the 70 disciples (Lk. 10.1-20; cf. the 70 elders, Num. 11.24-30) and the twofold love command (Lk. 10.25-37; cf. Deut. 6.5; Lev. 19.18), among others.

4.5. *Jesus: The Royal Prophet*

Last, but not least, Luke portrays Jesus to be both prophet and king, that is, the royal prophet. He began his portrait of Jesus in the infancy narrative showing him born to be king (Lk. 1.5–2.41). He complemented this in the inauguration narrative showing Jesus to be anointed both as king

(Ps. 2.7) and prophet (Isa. 42.1). But from Jesus' baptismal reception onwards Luke portrays Jesus' public ministry exclusively in prophetic terms. It is only at the end, as Jesus approaches Jerusalem, the royal city, that the kingship theme of the infancy and inauguration narratives (Lk. 1–4) and the prophetic theme of Jesus' public ministry (Lk. 4–18) are permanently fused into the complementary portrait of Jesus as king-prophet.

After his lengthy portrait of Jesus as prophet in Galilee and neighboring regions (Lk. 4–18) Luke reintroduces the kingship theme as Jesus journeys to up Jerusalem to celebrate the Passover. Approaching Jericho a blind beggar calls out to him: 'Jesus, Son of David, have mercy on me!' (Lk. 18.37, 38). The title 'Son of David' echoes the angel's announcement in the infancy narrative: 'the Lord God will give Him the throne of His father David' (Lk. 1.32). But neither this, nor any similar title, has been assigned to Jesus subsequently to his baptism. It is only when Jesus approaches Jerusalem, David's city, that he is once again called David's son. Before leaving Jericho, and 'because He was near Jerusalem' (Lk. 19.11), Jesus identifies himself in terms of his royal birthright. He tells the crowd, which is charged with messianic fervor (Lk. 19.11b), a parable about 'a certain nobleman [who] went into a distant country to receive a kingdom for himself' (Lk. 19.12).

Having introduced the kingship theme in the environs of Jericho, Luke strengthens his portrait of Jesus as king once he arrives in Jerusalem. Jesus' Triumphal Entry into Jerusalem is—echoing Solomon's coronation many generations earlier (1 Kgs 1.38-40)—the entry of a newly crowned king (Lk. 19.29-40). The accompanying crowd acclaim him king in the language of the Passover Psalm: 'Blessed is the king who comes in the name of the Lord' (Lk. 19.38; Ps. 118.26). But whereas the Psalm speaks about 'the One' who comes in the name of the Lord, the Passover crowd acclaims Jesus as 'the King'. Later during the week leading up to the Passover Jesus questions them about their messianic expectations: 'How is it that they say the Christ is David's son?' (Lk. 20.41). Quoting Ps. 110.1 he next asks: 'David therefore calls Him "Lord", and how is He his son?' (Lk. 20.44). Further, Jesus is crucified under the superscription: 'This is the King of the Jews' (Lk. 23.38). Finally, Jesus is enthroned, 'exalted to the right hand of God' (Acts 2.33a), fulfilling the enthronement language of Ps. 110.1. Peter understands this to mean that 'God has made Him both Lord and Christ' (Acts 2.36).

Though Jesus is identified as 'King' from Jericho to Jerusalem, and he confirms that identification, he continues to minister as a prophet, and to be identified as a prophet. During his arrest the men who were holding Jesus in custody mocked him as prophet (as they would also mock him as king, crowning him with thorns). Luke reports: 'they blindfolded Him and were asking Him, saying, "Prophesy, who is the one who hit you?" ' (Lk. 22.64). After the resurrection two of his disciples identify him, not as the rejected king, but as the prophet, approved by God and the people, but rejected by the religious and political leaders (Lk. 24.19, 20). Finally, during the days of his resurrection appearances Jesus, who began his public ministry in Galilee as the Spirit-ful, Spirit-led and Spirit-empowered prophet, still speaks words inspired by the Spirit (Acts 1.2).

In different contexts in Acts, Luke shows Jesus to be both the anointed king and the anointed prophet. Jesus is the anointed king in the context of his crucifixion. Following the release of Peter and John by the Sanhedrin, the community reflects upon David's psalm about the nations, peoples, kings and rulers who 'were gathered together against the Lord, and against His Christ' (Acts 4.25, 26; Ps. 2.1, 2). They recognize that this has been fulfilled in Jesus when Herod, Pilate, the Gentiles and the peoples of Israel 'gathered together against Thy holy servant Jesus, whom Thou didst anoint' (Acts 4.27). But, as one would expect from reading Luke, Jesus is also the anointed prophet in the context of his public ministry. Peter witnesses to Cornelius and his household 'about how God anointed Him [Jesus] with the Holy Spirit and power, and how He went about doing good...for God was with Him' (Acts 10.38). These two references, the first about Jesus as the anointed king and the second about Jesus as the anointed prophet, remind the reader that at the end (but only at the end) Jesus functions not simply as the anointed king nor simply as the anointed prophet but as a fusion of the two—the royal prophet.

The Gospel portraits of Jesus are complex and varied. For example, for John, the evangelist, Jesus is the eternal Word, the one who came down from heaven and to whence he will return. He is, moreover, the I AM who performs miracles which are signs about himself. For the evangelist Mark, Jesus is successively Teacher, Prophet, Messiah and (rejected) King. For the evangelist Matthew, Jesus is the Davidic King and Moses-like teacher, and, for Luke, the historian, Jesus is pre-eminently Savior and Prophet.

Though all four writers portray Jesus as prophet, Luke emphasizes this function in Jesus' public ministry much more than the other three. As we have demonstrated, Luke portrays Jesus to be: (1) the eschatological prophet; (2) the anointed prophet; and (3) the charismatic prophet. Indeed, Luke portrays Jesus to be a prophet from first to last, from the inauguration of his ministry through to his resurrection. In particular, Luke portrays Jesus' ministry as prophet as summing up and fulfilling five prophetic motifs: (1) he is a prophet like Isaiah, but greater than Isaiah; (2) he is a prophet like Elijah, but greater than Elijah; (3) he is a rejected prophet, but more than a rejected prophet; (4) he is the prophet like Moses, but he is a prophet greater than Moses; and (5) he is the royal prophet, but greater than David. Of Luke's portrait of Jesus as prophet it can, indeed, be said: The whole is greater than the sum of its parts. Luke portrays Jesus to be a prophet without equal or rival, but not without successors, for Jesus concludes and caps his prophetic ministry by establishing his disciples as an eschatological community of Spirit-baptized prophets. In his absence they will minister by the same power of the Holy Spirit as he himself ministered by, and will, therefore, do the same works as he himself did.

Chapter 3

THE DISCIPLES: A COMPANY OF SPIRIT-BAPTIZED PROPHETS
(ACTS 1.12–2.41)*

The disciples relate to Jesus after the manner of the disciples of a contemporary rabbi, or, since Jesus is the anointed prophet, after the ancient manner of one of the prophets of old and the sons of the prophets. In fact, after his ascension the disciples reproduce and perpetuate Jesus' prophetic ministries. Luke reports this in Acts, which is for him the necessary sequel to his report about Jesus as the anointed prophet. Though the structure of the book of Acts is complex it has two main foci: in Acts 1.1–6.7 Luke focuses on the disciples as a community of charismatic prophets; in Acts 6.8–28.32 Luke focuses on the ministry of six charismatic prophets. These are Stephen, Philip, Barnabas, Agabus, Peter and Paul. In this chapter I will examine Luke's report about the origin of the charismatic or prophetic community (Acts 1.12–2.41). In the next chapter I will examine Luke's report about the acts of the charismatic or prophetic community (Acts 2.42–6.7). In Chapter 5 I will investigate Luke's report about the acts of the five charismatic prophets (Acts 6.8–12.24), and in Chapter 6 I will investigate Luke's report about the acts of Paul (Acts 12.25–28.31).

1. The Theophany of Pentecost

The feast of Pentecost, which is sandwiched between the spring feast of Passover and the fall Feast of Tabernacles, is the second of the three pilgrim festivals in Israel's liturgical calendar.[1] On the morning of that

* This chapter develops my earlier paper, 'Signs on the Earth Beneath', which was read at the Twenty-first Annual Meeting of the Society for Pentecostal Studies (Lakeland, FL, 1991).
1. For the regulations about these three festivals see Lev. 23.4-44; Num. 28.16–29.40. 'Pentecost' is the Greek name for the Feast of Weeks which was cele-

first Pentecost which followed the momentous Passover some 50 days earlier when Jesus the Nazarene, a prophet mighty in deed and word, was crucified, three dramatic signs burst upon the disciples when they gathered on the Temple Mount.[2] Luke reports:

> And suddenly there came from heaven a noise like a violent, rushing wind, and it filled the whole house where they were sitting. And there appeared to them tongues as of fire distributing themselves, and they rested on each one of them. And they were all filled with the Holy Spirit and began to speak with other tongues, as the Spirit was giving them utterance (Acts 2.2-4).

In the light of Israel's history the meaning of the first two signs, the metaphorical wind and fire would be self-evident signposts, both to the disciples and to the assembled crowd, that a theophany is happening.

brated 50 days after the Passover. It was an agricultural festival, and like the feasts of Passover and Atonement it was a day of convocation at the sanctuary. In the intertestamental literature the book of *Jubilees* anchors the feast in the covenants with Noah and Abraham (14.19-20). After 70 CE, the feast was associated with the giving of the Law at Sinai. For a full discussion see Edward Lohse, 'πεντηκοστή', in *TDNT*, VI, pp. 44-53.

2.   It is such a commonplace to identify the 'house' (οἶκος) where the disciples gathered on the day of Pentecost (Acts 2.2) with the 'upper room' where the apostles were staying (Acts 1.13) that interpreters often ignore the issue or else defend this identification by asserting that the term 'house' used on its own cannot mean the temple (I. Howard Marshall, *The Acts of the Apostles: An Introduction and Commentary* [TNTC; Grand Rapids: Eerdmans], p. 68). But commonplace though it is, the identification is almost certainly wrong. Several lines of evidence indicate that on the day of Pentecost the disciples gathered on the Temple Mount: (1) In Luke's Bible, and that of his readers, namely, LXX, οἶκος is used of the Davidic temple (e.g. 2 Sam. 7.5, 13 [LXX; 2 Kgdms 7.5, 13]; 1 Kgs 6–8 [LXX; 3 Kgdms 6–8]). (2) Quoting Isa. 56.7 and Jer. 7.11, Jesus identifies the Temple Mount as God's house (οἶκος, Lk. 19.46). (3) Luke never reports or implies that the 120 disciples stayed in the upper room. Rather, he explicitly identifies the upper room as the place where the apostles, that is, the 11 only, were staying (Acts 1.13). (4) In adjacent contexts both before and after his Pentecost narrative (Acts 2.1-41) Luke reports that the disciples were continually in the temple (Lk. 24.53), and met in the temple day by day (Acts 2.46). (5) This practice of meeting in the temple every day continued for approximately three years, apparently up to the time of Stephen's martyrdom (Acts 5.12, 42). This evidence that on the day of Pentecost the disciples have gathered in the temple is compelling, but such is the power of popular tradition that many careful scholars accept the upper room tradition contrary to the evidence.

The meaning of the third sign, the speaking with other tongues, would not be immediately self-evident to the multitude which had gathered in response to what they were seeing and hearing, and they were bewildered by this sign (Acts 2.6), were amazed and marveled (Acts 2.7), and continued in amazement and great perplexity (Acts 2.12). At an opportune moment Peter addresses the multitude, declaring that what they have just witnessed is that which was spoken of through the prophet Joel, who had announced a pouring out of the Spirit which would result in a universal gift of prophecy at the time when a theophany was happening. As God's spokesman he announced this theophany in the following language:

> And I will grant wonders in the sky above, and signs on the earth beneath, blood, and fire, and vapor of smoke. The sun shall be turned into darkness, and the moon into blood, before the great and glorious day of the LORD shall come (Acts 2.19-20).

In the context of Pentecost,[3] the wonder in the sky (literally, heaven above) is the 'noise like a violent, rushing wind' which came suddenly from heaven (Acts 2.2). Similarly, the sign on the earth beneath is the 'tongues as of fire' which distributed themselves and rested on each disciple (Acts 2.3). Further, the 'fire' of Pentecost is described in Joel's oracle by its effect, which is unreported by Luke, namely, 'Blood, and fire, and vapor of smoke' (Acts 2.19c). In other words, 'the sun was turned into darkness, and the moon into blood' (Acts 2.20a). Thus, Joel announced a scene with the morning sun to the east and the late-setting moon to the west which, when viewed through the unreported but implied smoke of the 'fire' of Pentecost, not only darkens these celestial luminaries but also makes them appear blood red to those on the Temple Mount.

---

3.   In general, interpreters are very reluctant to identify the wonders and signs which Joel announced with the three wonders and signs which Luke reports on the day of Pentecost (Acts 2.2-4). Rather, they attempt to relate the cosmic wonders and signs of Joel's announcement either to the events of Jesus' crucifixion, such as the darkening of the noonday sun (Lk. 23.44) or to the cosmic portents heralding the consummation of the last days (Rev. 6.1ff.). But these attempts are a counsel of despair, and the explicit 'this is that' perspective of Peter (Acts 2.16) ought to cause interpreters to identify the wonders and signs on the day of Pentecost with the wonders and signs which Joel announced.

The theophany on the Temple Mount on this day of Pentecost is not only described in Joel's oracle with amazing exactitude,[4] but it also strongly echoes the greatest theophany in Israel's history. This is the theophany at Mt Sinai when God gave the Law to Israel and established the people as his covenant people. Some three months before the giving of the Law the Israelites had celebrated that first Passover and Moses had led them out of Egypt (Exod. 12.1-28). Having then brought them through the Red Sea (Exod. 14.1-31) Moses led them through the desert, with stops in the wilderness of Shur (Exod. 15.22-26), at Elim (Exod. 15.27), the wilderness of Sin (Exod. 16.1-36) and Rephidim (Exod. 17.1–18.27). After they arrived by these stages at Mt Sinai, the mountain of God (Exod. 3.1) Moses prepared the people for a divine visitation, reporting to them, 'for on the third day the LORD will come down on Mount Sinai in the sight of the people' (Exod. 19.11). The narrative then describes the theophany:

> So it came about on the third day, when it was morning, that there were thunder and lightning flashes and a thick cloud upon the mountain and a very loud trumpet sound, so that all the people who were in the camp trembled. And Moses brought the people out of the camp to meet God, and they stood at the foot of the mountain. Now Mount Sinai was all in smoke because the Lord descended upon it in fire; and its smoke ascended like the smoke of a furnace, and the whole mountain quaked violently (Exod. 19.16-18).

This theophany is more than a great and violent display of fireworks. It establishes Israel as the covenant people of God. More specifically, in

---

4.   Contra Richard D. Israel, 'Joel 2.28-32 (3.1-5 MT): Prism of Pentecost', in Cecil M. Robeck, Jr (ed.), *Charismatic Experiences in History* (Peabody, MA: Hendrickson, 1985), pp. 2-14. He writes: 'One must say that the text of the Joel passage does not really accord well with the phenomena described in Acts 2.1-4. The only real point of contact is the reception of the Spirit, though even at this point, the word, "filled with the Spirit"' does not really tally with the effusion referred to by the Hebrew word for "pouring out". Note also that the accompanying phenomena of wind, tongues of fire, and speaking in tongues are not explained by the quotation of the Joel passage' (p. 11). The above exposition of Acts 2.17-21 is the answer to Israel's failure to observe the many, comprehensive and detailed points of contact between Acts 2.1-4 and Joel 2.28-32. Further, the points of contact between these two texts are far closer than between any other Old Testament prophecy about the giving of the Spirit and Luke's description of the phenomena described in Acts 2.1-4.

terms that are most appropriate for Israel as a theocratic nation, it establishes their mission or vocation—they are to be a kingdom of priests
and a holy nation (Exod. 19.6).

Though this theophany at Mt Sinai with its powerful and terrifying
presence of God remained unequaled in Israel's history, many generations later the prophet Elijah also experienced a theophany on this same
mountain of God. Having fled from Jezebel after his victory over the
prophets of Baal on Mt Carmel, Elijah eventually came to Horeb, the
mountain of God (1 Kgs 19.8). As he stood on the mountain before the
Lord:

> behold, the LORD was passing by! And a great and strong wind was
> rending the mountains and breaking in pieces the rocks before the
> LORD; but the LORD was not in the wind. And after the wind an earth-
> quake, but the LORD was not in the earthquake. And after the earth-
> quake a fire, but the LORD was not in the fire; and after the fire a sound
> of gentle blowing (1 Kgs 19.11-12).

As in the earlier theophany when God gave the Law to Israel at Mt
Sinai, the theophany of Elijah's experience includes both the earthquake
and the fire. To these is added a great and strong (i.e. violent) wind.

The theophany on the day of Pentecost, now many generations further along in Israel's history, echoes these two earlier theophanies in at
least three respects. First, like the earlier theophanies it is at the mountain of God, though in the case of Pentecost it is on the Temple Mount,
that is, Mt Zion, the other mountain of God.[5] Secondly, like the theophany when God gave the Law to Israel it follows the pattern: (a) the
Passover is celebrated; (b) there is then an interval of several weeks;
(c) there are specific days of preparation; and (d) the theophany itself
happens in the morning.

Events	Mt Sinai	Day of Pentecost
Passover	Exod. 12.21-28	Luke 22.1-28
Interval of Weeks	Exod. 19.1 3 months	Acts 1.3, approx. 6 weeks 40 days
Days of Preparation	Exod. 19.11 3 days	approx. 7 days
Theophany	Exod. 19.6-18, morning: thunder, lightning, fire and smoke	Acts 2.2-4, third hour: wind, fire (and smoke) and speaking in tongues

    5.   Horeb, or Mt Sinai, is identified as the Mountain of God in Exod. 3.1 and
1 Kgs 19.10. Similarly, Mt Zion is identified as the mountain of the LORD in Isa.
2.3; Mic. 4.1; and Zech. 8.3.

However, whereas the theophany at Mt Sinai established Israel as a kingdom of priests the theophany on the day of Pentecost establishes the disciples as a community of prophets. Thirdly, the theophany on the day of Pentecost combines the signs of these earlier theophanies: the noise of the violent, rushing wind echoes the violent wind of Elijah's experience, the fire echoes the fire of the earlier two, and the smoke echoes the smoke when God appeared on Mt Sinai before Israel at the giving of the Law.

These wonders and signs of the theophany of Pentecost, which echo the theophany at the giving of the Law at Mt Sinai, can only mean that what is happening on the day of Pentecost is not only as dramatic as, but also as significant as what happened at Mt Sinai. In other words, the creation of the disciples as a community of prophets is as epochal as the earlier creation of Israel as a kingdom of priests. That is, on the day of Pentecost, and for the second time in the history of his people, God is visiting his people on his holy mountain and mediating a new vocation for them—prophethood rather than royal priesthood.

2. *The Promise of Pentecost*

While the first two signs of the theophany—the wind and the fire— would have been as unexpected and startling to the disciples as they were to the multitude of worshipers, the actual pouring out of the Spirit would not have been unexpected. In fact, the disciples were awaiting the gift of the Holy Spirit, which they received on the day of Pentecost accompanied by such unexpected signs. They had been expecting the pouring out of the Spirit because, both before and after the resurrection, Jesus had promised that they would receive the Holy Spirit.

At various points during his public ministry Jesus made several promises to the disciples about the Holy Spirit. The first of these is in the context of Jesus encouraging his disciples to pray (Lk. 11.1-13). The ultimate encouragement is the contrast between earthly fathers and the heavenly Father on the midrashic principle of light and heavy (*qal waḥomer*).

> If you then, being evil, know how to give good gifts to your children, how much more shall your heavenly Father give the Holy Spirit to those who ask him? (Lk. 11.13).

Matthew reports this encouragement more generally as 'how much more shall your Father who is in heaven give what is good to those who ask Him?' (Mt. 7.11b). Two observations are pertinent to this encouragement to pray: (1) of all the good gifts which the Father gives, the Holy Spirit, in Luke's perspective, is the ultimate good gift; and (2) this gift of the Holy Spirit can be asked for, that is, prayed for. Not coincidently, the pouring out of the Holy Spirit on the day of Pentecost (Acts 2.1-21) is in the context where the disciples, as Luke reports, 'were continually devoting themselves to prayer' (Acts 1.14, cf. 8.15).

The second of these pre-resurrection promises is in the context of impending opposition, 'before the synagogues and the rulers and authorities' (Lk. 12.11). In this time of trial Jesus commands:

> Do not be anxious about how or what you should speak in your defense, or what you should say; for the Holy Spirit will teach you in that very hour what you ought to say (Lk. 12.12).

Here is the promise that the Holy Spirit will function as the counsel for the defense, specifically, that the disciples will have the inspiration of the Holy Spirit when they are called upon to defend themselves. Jesus renews this promise just before his crucifixion, saying, 'for I will give you utterance and wisdom which none of your opponents will be able to resist or refute' (Lk. 21.15). The first version of this promise is initially fulfilled in Peter's defense before the Sanhedrin, where filled with the Holy Spirit he answers questions about the healing of the lame man (Acts 4.8-12). The second version of this promise is initially fulfilled in Stephen, a man full of the Holy Spirit and wisdom (Acts 6.3). Luke reports that his opponents from the Synagogue of the Freedmen 'were unable to cope with the wisdom and the Spirit with which he was speaking' (Acts 6.10).

These promises about the Spirit which Jesus made at various points during his public ministry are rather imprecise in terms of their fulfillment. In contrast, the three promises about the Spirit which Jesus made after his death and resurrection are very precise and definite in terms of their fulfillment. The first of these is the promise of power. Prior to his ascension, as reported in the Gospel, Jesus commissioned his disciples: 'you are witnesses of these things' (Lk. 24.48). For their vocation as witnesses Jesus then announced:

> And behold, I am sending forth the promise of My Father upon you; but you are to stay in the city until you are clothed with power from on high (Lk. 24.49).

Several observations are to be made from this text: (1) in the larger context of Luke, 'the promise of the Father' can only be the promise of the Holy Spirit which the heavenly Father will give to the disciples when they ask, or pray for it (Lk. 11.13); (2) the fulfillment of this announcement, that is, that the disciples will be clothed with power, will happen in Jerusalem. There they remained and on the day of Pentecost they were clothed with the power to witness about the Christ; (3) the promise of power, on the one hand, means that the disciples will begin their ministry with the same power, by which Jesus began his ministry (Lk. 4.14) and which characterized his entire ministry, as a prophet mighty (literally, powerful) in works and word (Lk. 24.19; cf. Acts 2.22; 10.38). On the other hand, this promise of power is also an implicit promise of the Holy Spirit, for the Spirit will be the source of power for the disciples (Acts 1.8), just as it was Jesus' source of power (Lk. 4.14; Acts 10.38).[6]

The second of the post-resurrection promises of the Spirit reiterates the earlier announcement of John the Baptist that the Messiah, of whom he is the forerunner, will 'baptize with the Holy Spirit and fire'

---

6.   In his interpretation of the Lukan data Robert P. Menzies separates Spirit (πνεῦμα) and power (δύναμις). He asserts that for Luke πνεῦμα is the direct agent of prophetic inspiration alone and, separately, δύναμις is miracle working power (*Empowered for Witness*, p. 117). Specifically, '[Luke] take[s] great care not to associate the Spirit directly with healings and exorcisms' (p. 115). Additionally, 'when Luke uses the terms δύναμις and πνεῦμα together he has in mind a combination of prophetic speech *and* miracles of healing and exorcisms' (p. 114). But all of the Lukan data which Menzies marshals to defend his thesis, in fact, proves the contrary. For example, the programmatic inauguration narrative (Lk. 3.1–4.30) associates 'the power of the Spirit' (Lk. 4.14) as directly with Jesus' reception of the Spirit at the Jordan (Lk. 3.22) as it associates the fulness of the Spirit and the leading of the Spirit (Lk. 4.1) with his reception of the Spirit. Further, Luke associates both Jesus' 'works and words' with δύναμις (Lk. 24.19); that is, Jesus' entire prophetic ministry, not just his miraculous works, consists of empowered words and empowered works. In addition, when Peter describes Jesus as 'anointed with the Holy Spirit and power' and one who, 'went about doing good and healing all who were oppressed by the devil' (Acts 10.38) he teaches that the Spirit is directly associated with healings and exorcisms. What is true for Jesus' experience of πνεῦμα and δύναμις will similarly be true for the disciples' experience: they will receive power (δύναμις) when the Spirit (πνεῦμα) comes upon them (Acts 1.8). From Pentecost onwards Luke's narrative shows that the disciples witnessed by words empowered by the Spirit and by works empowered by the Spirit. To use Menzies's own terms, his interpretation is both 'strange' and overly 'nuanced'. Despite the exegetical dexterity by which he attempts to explicate Luke's data about πνεῦμα and δύναμις, Menzies misunderstands Luke's use of these two terms.

(Lk. 3.16). Jesus introduces this promise of the Spirit commanding the disciples 'not to leave Jerusalem, but to wait for what the Father had promised, "which," [He said], "you heard from Me" ' (Acts 1.4). Clearly, this second promise of the Spirit gives further specificity and definition to the 'promise of the Father'. In other words, the promise of the Father is not only a clothing with power, but also, at the same time, a baptism in the Spirit. As Jesus commands the disciples to remain in Jerusalem he tells them that they will be 'baptized with the Holy Spirit not many days from now' (Acts 1.5).

As with the first promise there are several observations to be made regarding this text. First, Jesus narrows the focus of John the Baptist's promise. John had declared:

> He Himself will baptize you in the Holy Spirit and fire. And His win-
> nowing fork is in His hand to clean out his threshing floor, and to gather
> the wheat into His barn; but He will burn up the chaff with unquenchable
> fire (Lk. 3.16b, 17).

As John announced it in terms of a harvest metaphor, this messianic baptizing with the Spirit will be both a blessing (to gather wheat into his barn) and a judgment (he will burn up the chaff with unquenchable fire). As Jesus announced it, in the experience of his disciples this imminent baptizing with the Spirit is exclusively in terms of blessing for in his promise to the disciples he does not repeat the 'baptizing with...fire' of John's announcement, which is the unquenchable fire of judgment. Second, this baptizing with the Holy Spirit will take place in Jerusalem and only a few days later.

This promise that the disciples will be baptized with the Spirit is fulfilled in the day of Pentecost, when Jesus pours out the Spirit (Acts 2.33) and the disciples are filled with the Holy Spirit (Acts 2.4). Many years later Peter explains to the brethren in Jerusalem the gift of the Spirit to Cornelius and his household (Acts 11.1-3), reporting:

> And as I began to speak, the Holy Spirit fell upon them, just as [He did]
> upon us at the beginning. And I remembered the word of the Lord, how
> He used to say, 'John baptized with water, but you shall be baptized with
> the Holy Spirit' (Acts 11.15, 16).

Peter then concludes: 'If God therefore gave to them the same gift as [He gave] to us also after believing in the Lord Jesus Christ, who was I that I could stand in God's way?' (Acts 11.17). Several conclusions fol- low from this:

1. A variety of terms can in appropriate contexts describe this baptizing with the Holy Spirit: (a) the promise of the Father (Acts 1.4, cf. 2.39, a promise of Spirit baptism); (b) filling with the Holy Spirit (Acts 2.4); (c) the Spirit 'poured out' (Acts 2.17, 33; 10.45); (d) the Holy Spirit 'fell upon' (Acts 10.44; 11.15); and (e) the gift of the Holy Spirit (Acts 2.38; 10.45; 11.17).

2. The sign of being baptized with the Spirit is speaking with other tongues (Acts 2.4, 10.46). Thus, where speaking with other tongues is reported, even where 'baptized with the Holy Spirit' terminology is not used, as in the report of the disciples at Ephesus (Acts 19.6), it signifies that a baptizing with the Spirit has taken place.

3. This baptizing with the Spirit is a gift, one for which, indeed, Jesus encouraged his disciples to pray for (Lk. 11.13).

4. In every case, not only for the disciples on that day of Pentecost, this baptizing with the Spirit, as the promise of the Father, is a clothing with power.

5. This baptizing of the Spirit is potentially universal, 'For the promise [i.e. of the gift of the Holy Spirit (2.38)] is for you and your children, and for all who are far off, as many as the Lord our God shall call to Himself' (Acts 2.39).[7] Luke illustrates the universal extension of

---

7.   Concerning Peter's promise that the gift of the Spirit is potentially universal (Acts 2.38, 39) Max Turner correctly observes: 'The nature of the gift of the Spirit promised to Christians in 2.38-39 is clear enough—it is Joel's gift of the Spirit of prophecy' (*Power from on High*, p. 349). Strangely, he also asserts that the gift of the Spirit of prophecy forms 'a single "conversion-initiation" unit with conversion and baptism' (p. 397). He also asserts that '[for Luke] beyond the ascension of Jesus the gift of the Spirit *becomes soteriologically necessary*—even for Jesus' band of disciples' (p. 435; his italics). In order to sustain this perspective, namely, that the gift of the Spirit of prophecy (Acts 2.38, 39) is part of a single conversion-initiation unit and, even for the disciples, is soteriologically necessary, Turner is forced to define 'salvation' so broadly that the term loses any actual theological significance. Thus:

> [Luke] sees the charismatic 'Spirit of prophecy' as serving the church and empowering its pastoral ministries ([*sic*] of those who serve tables in Acts 6.3, 5, as well as that of prophets (Acts 11.28; 21.4, 11 etc.), of teachers (Acts 9.31, 11.24; 15.32 etc.) and of elders/overseers (Acts 20.28), as well as its evangelism... Luke is also more like the Paul of 1 Cor. 2.6-16 and 2 Cor. 3.12-18 who regards the Spirit who reveals and grants wisdom as essential for that real Christian understanding of the Gospel which transforms human existence and leads to the life of sonship. For him (as for Paul and John, though differently) the Spirit of prophecy affords the whole charismatic dimension of revelation

the baptizing with the Holy Spirit by reporting the experiences of Cornelius and his household at Caesarea (Acts 10.44-48), and the disciples of John at Ephesus (Acts 19.6).

6. Based on the paradigm of Jesus' own anointing with the Spirit (Lk. 3.22; 4.18) this Spirit-baptism which the disciples will experience is their 'anointing' for ministry, not only consecrating them for their task as witnesses (Lk. 24.48; Acts 1.8), but also inaugurating that very witness.[8]

The third promise of the Spirit prior to Pentecost is the programmatic promise:

> but you shall receive power when the Holy Spirit has come upon you; and you shall be My witnesses both in Jerusalem, and in all Judea and Samaria, and even to the remotest part of the earth (Acts 1.8).

This promise is clearly the first post-resurrection promise of the Spirit (Lk. 24.49). In both Lk. 24.49 and Acts 1.8 there is the promise of power for the disciples' vocation of being witnesses. The latter promise (Acts 1.8), however, makes explicit what was implicit in the former

> and spiritual wisdom which makes the difference between the vibrant, joyful, worshipping and generously supportive messianic community and what went before. His enthusiasm for this new community allows him to see it as the Israel of fulfillment, and to some extent to fill in the rifts that emerge from a critical examination of the epistles with eirenic and partially idealizing summaries. The radical holiness and corporate unity of this community is actively promoted and vigilantly preserved by the Spirit (cf. Acts 5.1-10) and her disputes are settled in appropriately reconciliatory fashion and under the Spirit's influence (Acts 15.28). *All this is 'salvation' and the Spirit is necessary to it* (p. 445; italics added).

This description of the Spirit of prophecy as salvation is a case of 'illegitimate totality transfer' (James Barr, *The Semantics of Biblical Literature* [Oxford: Oxford University Press, 1960], p. 222). If according to Turner, 'salvation' is 'all this'—that is, that salvation means everything pertaining to the Spirit of prophecy—then the terms 'salvation' and 'the Spirit of prophecy' cease to mean anything at all.

8.   According to the interpretation which I have proposed the disciples' forthcoming Spirit-baptism is neither the purgative act of messianic judgment (Dunn, *Baptism in the Holy Spirit*, p. 11); nor is it the sifting and separating work of the Spirit through Spirit-empowered witness (Menzies, *Empowered for Witness*, p. 127); nor is it the cleansing of Israel, restoring it as utopian Zion (Turner, *Power from on High*, p. 183). In comparison to these interpretations, my interpretation has the advantage that it relates it to the disciples' actual and immediate experience on the day of Pentecost rather than to some more ultimate result for Israel that only begins on the day of Pentecost.

promise (Lk. 24.49), namely, that the Holy Spirit is the source of power for witness. Therefore, all the observations that were made for the former promise apply to the latter as well. We may add here by way of emphasis, however, that this promise of power applies both to Spirit-inspired witness, such as Peter gave on the day of Pentecost (note the verb ἀποφθέγγομαι in Acts 2.4, 14) and also to Spirit-empowered miracles, such as Luke reports of the apostles immediately following his Pentecost narrative (Acts 2.43). In other words, just as Jesus, because he had been anointed with the Spirit, was a prophet who was powerful in both works and word (Lk. 24.19), so the disciples, because they will be baptized with the Spirit, will be prophets who will be powerful in both works and word. Conscious of this dual works and word dimension of power the disciples could pray: '[that] signs and wonders take place through the name of thy holy servant Jesus' (Acts 4.30b). Luke reports that in answer to this prayer, the disciples 'were all filled with the Holy Spirit, and began to speak the word of God with boldness' (Acts 4.31b). He then sums up this dual works and word witness about the resurrection of the Lord Jesus: 'and abundant grace was upon them all' (Acts 4.33).

We can now sum up this survey of Jesus' promises of Pentecost. The three pre-resurrection promises promise the disciples the Spirit somewhat imprecisely: first, as a gift to be prayed for; and secondly, as the source of a Spirit- and Wisdom-inspired defense when they are on trial. The three post-resurrection promises, more immediately and specifically, promise the Spirit in Jerusalem in a few days as (1) a clothing with power; (2) a baptizing with the Holy Spirit; and (3) receiving power when the Holy Spirit comes on them. Though the latter three promises of Pentecost are more immediate and specific in their fulfillment, the vocation which their fulfillment effects is implicit and somewhat ill-defined. It is Joel's oracle which Peter quotes to explain the baptizing of the Spirit which the disciples have just experienced which gives explicit and ultimate definition to the pouring out of the Spirit on the day of Pentecost—it establishes them as a community of charismatic prophets.

3. *Inaugurating the Prophethood of All Believers*

As we have seen, on the day of Pentecost Jesus pours out the same Spirit, who had earlier anointed him and empowered his ministry, upon his disciples to baptize them and empower their ministry as his successors. In this way, just as Jesus was the Spirit-anointed prophet, so the disciples, as heirs and successors to his prophetic ministry, become a community of Spirit-baptized prophets, the prophethood of all believers.

The three signs which Luke reports on the day of Pentecost (Acts 2.2-4) are appropriate for this epochal event in the history of salvation. The first two signs—the signs of theophany, that is, the metaphorical wind and the fire—signify that God is once again visiting his people as he had earlier visited them at Mt Sinai when he formed them into 'a kingdom of priests and a holy nation' (Exod. 19.5). The third sign—'they were all filled with the Holy Spirit and began to speak with other tongues as the Spirit was giving them utterance' (Acts 2.4)—signifies that in addition to the actual theophany, and in fulfillment of the promises that the Holy Spirit would be given to the disciples (Lk. 24.49; Acts 1.5, 8), Jesus has poured out the Spirit, transferring the Spirit from himself to them.

Not surprisingly, it is the sign of the pouring out of the Spirit, rather than the two signs of theophany, which is the center of the crowd's response to the things which it sees and hears. Luke reports:

> And when this sound occurred, the multitude came together, and were bewildered, because they were each one hearing them speak in his own language. And they were amazed and marveled, saying, 'Why, are not all these who are speaking Galileans? And how is it that we each hear [them] in our own language to which we were born?' (Acts 2.6-8).

After reporting the various nations represented in the crowd Luke summarizes their response, writing, 'And they all continued in great amazement and great perplexity, saying to one another, "what does this mean?"' (Acts 2.12). Though the full meaning of the third sign awaits Peter's explanation, Luke's description of the disciples' reception of the Spirit, namely, 'they were all filled with the Holy Spirit' (Acts 2.4), gives Luke's readers two clues to its meaning.

'Filled with the Holy Spirit' is a term which Luke has appropriated from LXX, the Greek language translation of the Hebrew Scriptures. It occurs five times in LXX. The first three times are in the context of the manufacture of the High Priest's garments and the construction of the Tabernacle. In this context God fills the artisans, such as Bezalel and his co-workers, with 'the Spirit of perception' or with 'a divine spirit of wisdom and understanding' (Exod. 28.3; 31.3; 35.31). For these artisans the Spirit of wisdom is the Spirit who imparts wisdom, a wisdom which is manual skill or craftsmanship. The fourth occurrence of the term is in reference to Joshua. As the successor to Moses Joshua is 'filled with the Spirit of knowledge' (Deut. 34.9). Thus, just as Moses was a charismatic leader (Num. 11.17), so Joshua, his successor, would also be a charismatic leader. The final occurrence of the term is the promise that the enigmatic 'Shoot...from the stem of Jesse', upon whom rests the sevenfold Spirit of the Lord, will be filled with 'the spirit of wisdom and understanding, the spirit of counsel and strength, the spirit of knowledge and the fear of the Lord' (Isa. 11.3). In all five of these occurrences, the term 'filled with the Spirit', whether it describes manual craftsmanship on the one hand, or leadership skills on the other hand, invariably describes a charismatic activity of the Holy Spirit.

In addition to this Septuagintal background, which is implicit in his appropriation of the term 'filled with the Spirit', Luke has also already used the term three times in his 'first account...about all that Jesus began to do and teach' (Acts 1.1). He uses it for the first time when he reports that the son who is soon to be born to Zacharias and Elizabeth 'will be filled with the Holy Spirit while yet in his mother's womb' (Lk. 1.15). He uses the term for the second time when he describes Elizabeth, John's mother, as 'filled with the Holy Spirit' (Lk. 1.41) and he uses it for the third time when he reports that Zacharias, John's father, 'was filled with Holy Spirit and prophesied' (Lk. 1.67). From these three texts we can draw two conclusions about the way Luke uses the term, 'X was filled with Holy Spirit'. In the first place, as in the case of John, son of Zacharias and Elizabeth, Luke uses the term to describe a general prophetic ministry (note Lk. 1.76; 20.8), with no limitations to the time of that ministry nor any indication of any phenomena which might be associated with that ministry. In the second place, as in the cases of Zacharias, explicitly, and Elizabeth, implicitly, Luke uses the term as an introductory formula to describe a moment of prophetic inspiration. Thus, 'filled with the Holy Spirit' is the introductory formula, and the direct speech which follows is a pneuma discourse, that is, prophecy inspired by the Spirit.

Luke's report of the third sign on the day of Pentecost conforms to this characteristic Lukan use of the term. His report, 'And they [the disciples] were all filled with the Holy Spirit' (Acts 2.4a) is the introductory formula which announces prophetic speech. The sign 'and [they] began to speak with other tongues, as the Spirit was giving them utterance' (Acts 2.4b) is an outburst of prophecy. Peter's subsequent address to the crowd (Acts 2.14-36) is the pneuma discourse—speech inspired by the Holy Spirit. This is confirmed by two observations. First, Luke's narrative follows the pattern: introductory formula (Acts 2.4) followed by a report of direct speech (Acts 2.14ff.); and secondly, Luke uses the verb ἀποφθέγγομαι to introduce Peter's Pentecost address in 2.14, the same verb which he used in Acts 2.4 to describe the Spirit inspiring the disciples. This repetition is necessary because Luke has separated his introductory formula, 'filled with the Holy Spirit' (Acts 2.4) from his pneuma discourse (Acts 2.14-36) by a report of the crowd's response to the third sign (Acts 2.5-13). Peter's pneuma discourse has three sections: (1) an explanation of the signs of Pentecost (Acts 2.14-21); (2) a witness to Jesus as Lord and Christ (Acts 2.22-36); and (3) an exhortation to the crowd to repent and be saved (Acts 2.37-41). The first section alone, that is, Peter's explanation of the signs, is pertinent to the subject of this chapter. Having already focused on that part of Joel's text which explains the first two signs, namely Acts 2.19-21, we will now focus on that part of Joel's text which explains the third sign, namely, Acts 2.17, 18.

In answering the question of the crowd—'What does this mean?' (Acts 2.12)—and in refuting the mocking charge of some—'they are full of sweet wine' (Acts 2.13)—Peter, inspired by the Spirit, prophetically declared (note Luke uses the verb ἀποφθέγγομαι in both Acts 2.4 and 2.14):

> but this is what was spoken of through the prophet Joel:
> And it shall be in the last days, God says,
> That I will pour forth of my Spirit upon all humankind;
> and your sons and daughters shall prophesy,
> and your young men shall see visions,
> and your old men shall dream dreams;
> even upon my bondslaves, both men and women,
> I will in those days pour forth of my Spirit
> And they shall prophesy (Acts 2.16-18).

By quoting this oracle from Joel and applying it as the explanation of being filled with the Holy Spirit and speaking with other tongues, Peter makes three points: (1) the pouring out of the Holy Spirit is the eschatological gift of the Spirit; (2) the pouring out of the eschatological gift of the Spirit is the Spirit of prophecy; and (3) the pouring out of the eschatological Spirit of prophecy is for the community of God's people.

First, Peter indicates that the pouring out of the Spirit, which the disciples have just experienced, is the eschatological gift of the Spirit by peshering, or contemporizing, Joel's somewhat imprecise, 'after these things' (Joel 2.28), to the definite, 'in the last days' (Acts 2.17). By using the term 'in the last days', Peter is appropriating the familiar terminology of the two-age historiography of contemporary Judaism, namely, the 'former days' and the 'latter days'. In contemporary Jewish historiography the latter days, or last days, are the age of the Messiah and the complementary gift of the Holy Spirit. Earlier, at Caesarea Philippi Peter had confessed that Jesus was 'the Christ [i.e. Messiah] of God' (Lk. 9.20), and later on that day of Pentecost would declare that 'God has made him [this Jesus whom they had crucified] both Lord and Christ' (Acts 2.36). In addition to the coming of Jesus, he the Messiah, has also (necessarily) poured out the complementary gift of the Spirit. Therefore, in contemporizing the oracle of Joel Peter is affirming to the temple crowd that the pouring out of the Spirit, which they have just witnessed, demonstrates that the age of the Messiah, the last days, has already been inaugurated. As Luke's readers well know, the Messianic age was inaugurated a generation earlier in the complementary outburst of prophecy and the birth of Jesus, which Luke reported in his infancy narrative (Lk. 1.5–2.38).

Secondly, Peter indicates that this eschatological pouring out of the Spirit is the pouring out of the Spirit of prophecy. In other words, Joel's oracle identifies the disciples' experience of 'speaking in other tongues as the Spirit gave utterance' (Acts 2.4) to be prophetic speech. The prophetic character of this eschatological gift of the Spirit is reinforced by Joel's reference to dreams and visions, which, from the time of Moses, are the accredited media of prophetic revelation (cf. Num. 12.6). Peter emphasizes the prophetic character of the gift of the Spirit by adding the summarizing statement, 'And they shall prophesy' (Acts 2.18) to Joel's oracle.

Thirdly, the pouring out of the eschatological Spirit of prophecy is for the community of God's people. In the former days the charismatic gifts of the Spirit, including prophecy, were restricted to chosen leaders. In contrast to the former days, in these last days the gift of the Spirit of prophecy is for all humankind. In the context of Joel's oracle this is the promise of the pouring out of the Spirit of prophecy upon the entire nation. As Peter will make clear later on the day of Pentecost, however, it is only upon those who repent (Acts 2.38), not upon the nation irrespective of their spiritual condition. When God had earlier transferred his Spirit from Moses to the 70 elders and they prophesied, Moses had declared, 'Would that all the Lord's people were prophets, and that the Lord would put His Spirit upon them' (Num. 11.30). The pouring out of the Spirit on the disciples on the day of Pentecost fulfills, in part, that earnest desire, for as Joel's oracle announces it 'all humankind' means sons and daughters, young men and old men and bondslaves, both men and women. Thus, the age of the Messiah, the last days, is characterized by a universal pouring forth of the Spirit of prophecy which crosses all age, gender and socio-economic barriers in contrast to Israel's experience in the former days when only selected individuals were endowed with the Spirit. What Joel's oracle announced for the some time in the future actually happened on the day of Pentecost when both men and women, some younger, such as Jesus' brothers, and some older, such as Jesus' mother, prophesy. (Note that the antecedent of 'they' [Acts 2.1] is the 120 disciples [Acts 1.14], not the 12.) This community outburst of prophecy, which fulfills Joel's oracle, had an earlier fulfillment in Luke's narrative when sons and daughters (John, Mary), the young and the old (John, Zecharias, Simeon, Anna and Elizabeth) and bondslaves (Mary, Simeon) became the prophetic precursors to Pentecost.

In Luke's theology, the day of Pentecost is a momentous and epochal episode in the forward movement of the history of salvation. It is the climax to the generation-long turning of the ages (Lk. 1–2; Acts 2). It is the consummation of former days and the full inauguration of the latter days. The sound of the violent wind from heaven which was heard on the Temple Mount that day and the appearance of the tongues of fire are the signs of the theophany which effects a new reality in the people of God—a community-wide pouring out of the Spirit of prophecy. This pouring out of the Spirit of prophecy is neither the birth of the Church, nor merely a blessing for God's people. Rather, as the promises of Pentecost compel us to conclude, it is vocational, that is, it baptizes and empowers the company or community of God's people to witness as prophets about the arrival of the Messiah and the new age which his arrival has inaugurated. Thus, the pouring out of the Spirit on the day of Pentecost inaugurates nothing less than God's people as the prophethood of all believers. Luke's Pentecost narrative reports this inauguration of the prophethood of all believers and, in his narratival strategy, becomes programmatic for the ministry of the disciples as an ever growing company of prophets. This Luke subsequently narrates.

Chapter 4

THE ACTS OF THE COMMUNITY OF PROPHETS (ACTS 2.42–6.7)

Jesus completed his redemptive ministry by giving orders to his disciples by the Holy Spirit about their imminent Spirit-baptism and empowering (Acts 1.2, 5, 8). Having ascended to heaven he then poured out the Spirit upon the disciples on the day of Pentecost (Acts 2.33). He thereby transferred the anointing and empowering Spirit from himself to them, just as the Lord had earlier transferred the Spirit from Moses to the 70 elders, from Saul to David, and from Elijah to Elisha. By this act of transferring the Spirit to his disciples, Jesus, the Spirit-anointed prophet, makes his disciples a community of Spirit-baptized prophets. This fulfills an ancient oracle of the prophet Joel about a future age of restoration and blessing when the entire nation or community of God's people, irrespective of age, gender or social status, would have the Spirit poured out upon them. Thus, on the day of Pentecost Jesus inaugurated the prophethood of all believers. Following his report of this amazing event Luke will next report the acts of this community of Spirit-baptized prophets.

1. *The Community of Prophets Becomes a Nation*

Luke will soon shift the focus of his narrative from the acts of the community of Spirit-baptized prophets (Acts 2.42–6.7) to the acts of six charismatic leaders, beginning with Stephen and ending with Paul (Acts 6.8–28.31). Because not only Joel's oracle, but also its fulfillment on the day of Pentecost is about a community of prophets, Luke, of necessity, must first report the acts of this prophetic community before shifting his focus to individual members of the prophetic community. Luke highlights the community aspect/phenomenon of Spirit-baptism/inspiration by discussing incidents involving increasingly large groups of believers. In Acts Luke opens his reporting about the eleven apostles, who have a twelfth apostle added in those few days between the ascension of Jesus and the day of Pentecost (Acts 1.2, 13, 26). Soon, however, the focus shifts to a company of about 120 persons, who include some women, Mary the mother of Jesus, and his brothers (Acts 1.14-15). Before the day of Pentecost is over the number swells by about 3000 (Acts 2.41). As the apostles continue to witness in Jerusalem the number of men comes to be about 5000 (Acts 4.4). At this point Luke stops counting and describes the believers simply as 'the multitude' (Acts 4.32). Finally Luke identifies the followers of Jesus as the Church (τὴν ἐκκλησιαν, Acts 5.11), the term whose first appearance in Scripture describes Israel as a nation (LXX; Deut. 4.10; 9.10; 18.16). Therefore, at this point in his narrative Luke borrows a term from the Septuagint to portray the growing community of prophets as having achieved the status of nationhood, theologically if not fully numerically. Significantly, the community of prophets has grown from a company of 120 on the day of Pentecost to a nation of prophets, true heirs and successors to Israel as a nation of priests. Having achieved the status of nationhood, the growth in the number of disciples continues. Thus, Luke reports further that a multitude of men and women were added (Acts 5.14). Indeed, Luke's narrative on the acts of the community or nation of prophets concludes with the triumphant report: 'And the word of God kept on spreading; and the number of the disciples continued to increase greatly in Jerusalem, and a great many of the priests were becoming obedient to the faith' (Acts 6.7).

As we have observed above, Luke delays using the term τὴν ἐκκλησιαν or 'church'—the term which first and foremost in Scripture meant the people of God gathered as a nation—until late in his narrative about the acts of the disciples as a community of prophets. There are two primary factors in this delay. The first factor is quantitative or numerical and is related to the explosive growth of the community of disciples from its very small beginnings. In the context of Joel, however, the future pouring out of the Spirit is upon 'all flesh', that is, upon God's people as a nation. This promise is initially fulfilled in Luke's infancy narrative in the persons of representative individuals, from John to Anna, who herald the coming of the Christ, or Messiah, and renew the gift of prophecy within the nation. In turn, these representatives of the restoration of prophecy are, themselves, precursors to the pouring out of the Spirit of prophecy on the day of Pentecost on the company of disciples, who number about 120. But while the 120 constitute a true community of prophets they do not, in themselves, connote a nation, except potentially. It is not until the potential begins to be realized after the size of the community has risen beyond 5000 men to number a multitude that Luke terms God's people τὴν ἐκκλησιαν, that is, a nation or Church.

The second factor in Luke's delay in using the term τὴν ἐκκλησιαν is that the experience of the disciples must conform to, or catch up to, the theology of Pentecost, as it has been mediated through the prophet Joel. In other words, since Joel announced the pouring out of the Spirit of prophecy upon the nation, Luke cannot use the term 'nation' until there has been a nationwide experience of prophecy. This very thing happens following the release of Peter and John by the Sanhedrin and their subsequent return to the community of disciples and report to them (Acts 4.23-31). Luke reports:

> And when they had prayed, the place where they had gathered together was shaken, and they were all filled with the Holy Spirit, and [began] to speak the word of God with boldness (Acts 4.31).

Several observations need to be made concerning Luke's report about the experience of the community. First, the antecedent for the phrases 'they had gathered together' and 'they were all filled with the Holy Spirit' is Luke's earlier reference in the same chapter to the 5000 men who have believed (Acts 4.4). Thus, Luke informs Theophilus and all subsequent readers of his narrative that over 5000 men were filled with the Holy Spirit.

Secondly, though Luke does not identify it at this point, the place (τόπος) where they have gathered was surely the Temple Mount,[1]

---

1. Contra Ernest Haenchen, *The Acts of the Apostles: A Commentary* (trans. Bernard Noble and Gerald Shinn; Philadelphia: Westminster Press, 1971), who, commenting on 4.23, writes: 'When Luke speaks of the community assembled for worship or deliberation, he sees in his mind's eye not the great numbers he used in 2.41 and 4.4 to illustrate the divine blessing that lay on the community, but the band of believers gathered in *one room* which he was accustomed to see around him in the services of his own congregation' (p. 226; italics added). Similarly, Marshall, *Acts*, writes without explanation: 'The *room* in which the disciples were gathered shook as if an earthquake were taking place' (p. 107; italics added). Both of these commentators negate the possibility that Luke is reporting a theophany on the Temple Mount accompanied by a nationwide pouring forth of the Spirit of prophecy. Restricting the disciples and place to a gathering in a room, as they do, not only ignores the parallels between this narrative and the Pentecost narrative but also

which would readily accommodate gatherings numbering thousands more than this.[2] This conclusion is supported by four adjacent texts in Luke's narrative. Earlier Luke has reported that after the resurrection the disciples were continually in the temple, praising God (Lk. 24.53), and that after the day of Pentecost Peter and John went up to the temple to pray (Acts 3.1). Further, subsequent to the events which Luke reports in Acts 4, the disciples were still 'all with one accord in Solomon's portico' (Acts 5.12), and they continued to meet 'every day in the temple' (5.42). This identification of the 'place' (τόπος) where they had gathered as the Temple Mount is confirmed by the fact that in the narrative which immediately follows the temple is twice described by the same term τόπος, as Luke has used in 4.31 (Acts 6.13, 14; cf. 21.28).

Thirdly, Luke describes this immense company of disciples who have gathered as being 'all filled with the Holy Spirit'. This is the sixth time Luke has used the term, 'filled with the Holy Spirit' in his two-volume narrative about the origin and spread of Christianity (Lk. 1.15, 41, 67; Acts 2.4; 4.8, 31). As we have seen, Luke uses the term consistently and explicitly as an introductory formula for prophets or prophesying (e.g. Lk. 1.67; Acts 2.4, 17). Therefore, filled with the Holy Spirit, this immense company of disciples gathered together on the Temple Mount all prophesy; that is, speak the word of God boldly. In other words, their Spirit-filled witness is as much inspired prophecy as was Peter's Spirit-filled witness on the day of Pentecost. Thus, Luke has reported nothing less than a nationwide outburst of prophesying.

Fourthly, accompanying this nationwide outburst of prophesying Luke reports that 'the place where they had gathered together was shaken'. In light of the clear echoes of the Mt Sinai and Elijah theophanies with which Luke describes the theophany on the day of Pentecost it is evident that the shaking of the Temple Mount this day also echoes the shaking reported for those same earlier Mt Sinai and Elijah theophanies (Exod. 19.18; 1 Kgs 19.11). Therefore, just as the Spirit-filling of the disciples on the day of Pentecost was accompanied by a theo-

---

ignores both the fact that the disciples met on the Temple Mount every day (Acts 2.46; 5.42) and that Luke uses the term 'place' (τόπος) to describe the temple (Acts 6.13, 14), not some 'room'.

2.   Joachim Jeremias, *Jerusalem in the Time of Jesus* (trans. F.H. Cave and C.H. Cave; London: SCM Press, 1969), p. 82, calculates that 6400 men, each with an animal for sacrifice, could gather on the Temple Mount at one time. A substantially larger crowd could gather when they did not bring animals for sacrifice.

phany, so the Spirit-filling of this assembled company of thousands of disciples is also accompanied by a theophany.

These four observations lead to the inescapable conclusion that in this narrative Luke is describing a corporate outburst of prophecy among all of God's people, who number in the thousands. Luke has thus reported the actual historical fulfillment of Moses' earnest desire: 'Would that all the Lord's people were prophets, that the Lord would put His Spirit upon them!' (Num. 11.29). Therefore, after and because of this massive outburst of prophecy it is appropriate to call the disciples, τὴν ἐκκλησιαν, that is, nation or Church, in a way that it is not appropriate to describe the individuals in the infancy narrative who prophesy, or the company of disciples on the day of Pentecost who also prophesy. Here in Luke's narrative, for the first time ever in the redemptive history of God's people, those people truly function as a nation of prophets—the prophethood of all believers.

2. Programmatic Summary: Characteristics of the Prophetic Community (2.42-47)

Following the Pentecost narrative (Acts 2.1-41) Luke gives a summary of the disciples, who, as he has just described, have become a community of prophets by virtue of the pouring out of the Holy Spirit. This summary is not a concluding summary, as for example, will be found in Acts 6.7, among others, but it is a programmatic summary. This type of summary is to be found in the historical books of the Old Testament, whose historiography influences Luke's own historiography. For example, Acts 1 and 2 show several structural affinities with Judges 1 and 2. First, both Judges and Acts report the history of a new (that is, a second) generation of God's people following respectively the narrative history of the first generation of Israel which entered the land under Joshua's leadership, and the origin of Christianity in the person and ministry of Jesus. Secondly, both Judges and Acts begin with a narrative which recapitulates final episodes reported in the previous books, Joshua and Luke, respectively. Thirdly, both Judges and Acts next give programmatic summaries which introduce themes to be developed in the remainder of the book. In Judges the programmatic summary is found in Judg. 2.11-23. It introduces a fourfold thematic cycle of Israel's history, often summarized by the popular alliterative device: (1) sin—'the sons of Israel did evil in the sight of the Lord and served the Baals' (Judg. 2.11); (2) servitude—'the Lord gave them into the hands of plunderers who plundered them' (Judg. 2.13); (3) supplication—'the Lord was moved to pity by their groaning' (Judg. 2.18b); and (4) salvation—'the Lord raised up judges who delivered them from the hands of those who plundered them' (Judg. 2.16). This editorial summary is programmatic for the six reports of judges which follow, beginning with Othniel, son of Kenaz (Judg. 3.7-12) and concluding with Samson (Judg. 13.16-31). Similarly in Acts 2.42-47 Luke gives his readers a programmatic summary which introduces for his readers the narrative of the acts of this eschatological community of prophets.

Luke's programmatic summary introduces his readers first to the inner life of the prophetic community. By 'inner life of the community' I mean the attitudes and practices of the disciples as a community of prophets, not the interior personal spirituality of individual disciples. Describing the inner life of the disciples, who now number more than 3000 (Acts 2.41), Luke writes: 'And they were continually devoting themselves to the apostles's teaching and to fellowship, to the breaking of bread and to prayer' (Acts 2.42). Unity is a corollary to these features (Acts 2.46; 4.32; 5.12).

Secondly, Luke's programmatic summary introduces his readers to the outer life of the prophetic community. By 'outer life of the community', I mean the community in its witness about Jesus to those who are not disciples. Describing the outer life of the community Luke writes: 'And everyone kept feeling a sense of awe; and many wonders and signs were taking place through the apostles' (Acts 2.43). In addition to this witness by power there is also the witness of the word, as in Peter's witness after the lame man was healed (Acts 3.11-26), or the two reports of witness before the Sanhedrin (Acts 4.8-22; 5.17-42). Growth in the number of disciples is a corollary to these features (Acts 2.47; 4.4; 5.14; 6.1).

Beginning with the witness by work and word resulting from the healing of the lame man at the Beautiful Gate of the temple (Acts 3.1-26) through to the problem of broken fellowship concerning the distribution of food among the Hellenistic and Hebrew widows (Acts 6.1-7), Luke will develop these complementary themes of the inner and outer life of the Church. He does this by narrating a combination of specific examples which illustrate one or more aspects of the themes and by giving periodic summaries. Since Luke's report on the acts of the community of prophets covers a period of approximately three years this combination of example and summary shows the regular or normal inner and outer life of the Church, rather than the unusual and rare life of the Church.

2.1. *The Inner Life of the Community of Prophets*

In his programmatic summary Luke identifies four aspects or characteristics of the inner life of the prophetic community: (1) the apostles' teaching; (2) fellowship; (3) the breaking of bread; and (4) prayer. The first characteristic of the inner life of the Church is that the disciples, now numbering over 3000, 'were continually devoting themselves to the apostles' teaching' (Acts 2.42a). Clearly, the apostles, as Spirit-baptized prophets first function as teachers. This parallels Jesus' own ministry, where, following his anointing by the Spirit, Jesus returned to Galilee, 'in the power of the Spirit... And he [began] teaching in all their synagogues and was praised by all' (Lk. 4.14b-15). In this programmatic report about Jesus, Luke juxtaposes two prophetic themes, power and teaching, that is, ministry in work and word. And so it is no surprise that in the synagogue in Capernaum, Jesus not only amazes the crowd by teaching with authority (Lk. 4.31-32) but amazes the crowd by commanding the unclean spirits with power and authority (Lk. 4.36). Similarly, Luke reports on a subsequent occasion that one day as he was teaching, 'the power of the Lord was [present] for Him to perform healing' and he healed a paralyzed man (Lk. 5.17-26). Furthermore, at the house of Simon the Pharisee, Simon identifies Jesus as a prophet (Lk. 7.39) and also as a teacher (Lk. 7.40). After the apparently crushing end to Jesus' ministry by the crucifixion, two of this disciples reiterate these complementary themes by referring to him as a prophet mighty or powerful in works and word. In the same way, then, that Jesus, the anointed prophet, taught from first to last, the disciples also, as Spirit-baptized prophets, continually taught those who were added to the community of disciples.

Luke does not report the content of the apostles' teaching to which the disciples were continually devoting themselves. Nevertheless, it would have followed the outline which Luke has just reported in Peter's Pentecost sermon. Here Peter has witnessed about:

> Jesus the Nazarene, a man attested to you by God with miracles and wonders and signs which God performed through Him in your midst, just as you yourselves, know—this [Man], delivered up by the predetermined plan and foreknowledge of God, you nailed to a cross by the

hands of godless men and put [Him] to death. And God raised Him up
again, putting an end to the agony of death, since it was impossible for
him to be held in its power (Acts 2.22-24).

Luke's brief synopsis of Peter's witness reports three aspects of his
teaching about Jesus: (1) his public ministry of miracles; (2) his rejection by the Jews and subsequent crucifixion by the Romans; and (3) his
resurrection. In other words, the apostles taught those things which are
recorded in the Gospels. In fact, Mark, who was Peter's interpreter
(Eusebius, *Eccl. Hist.* 2.15.12), followed the same fundamental threefold structure. When Luke, however, writes about the apostles' teaching
in his programmatic summary he undoubtedly has in mind his own
narrative about 'all that Jesus began to do and teach'.

Secondly, the fledgling prophetic community continually devoted
themselves to fellowship—κοινωνία. The word κοινωνία is a *hapax
legomen* in Luke–Acts, that is, Luke uses it but one time. In fact,
κοινός root words are rare in Luke's writings. Thus, in Luke 5.10 Luke
uses κοινός to describe James and John as fishing partners of Peter.
This fellowship which characterized the inner life of the prophetic
community is defined in Acts 2.44 as the community's having 'all
things in common'. Specifically, this means that 'they [began] selling
their property and possessions, and were sharing them with all, as any-
one might have need' (Acts 2.45). Thus, to Luke, fellowship is concrete. It is a matter of sharing property and possessions (cf. Acts 4.32-
35).

Luke reports two representative examples of this common practice of
fellowship, or sharing of property and possessions. The first example is
a certain Joseph, 'a Levite of Cyprian birth who was also called Barnabas by the apostles' (Acts 4.37). This Barnabas is a positive example
of fellowship. Owning a tract of land, he 'sold it and laid it at the
apostles' feet' (Acts 4.38). From the many possible positive examples
of fellowship, Luke reports about Barnabas because the latter will
reappear in the narrative as (1) a companion of the newly converted
Saul (Acts 9.26, 30); (2) a minister in Antioch (Acts 11.22-26); and
(3) the prophet and teacher who will accompany Paul on his first mis-
sionary journey (Acts 13.1–15.36), which begins in Cyprus, Barnabas's
native land. The second example of fellowship concerns a certain man
named Ananias, and his wife Sapphira (Acts 5.1-11). This married
couple provide a negative example of fellowship. Like Barnabas they
sold a piece of land. Unlike Barnabas they kept back some of the price

for themselves, while bringing the remainder to the apostles and pretending that it was the full price of the land (Acts 5.2-4). Both are struck dead for lying to the Holy Spirit (Acts 5.3), or for testing the Spirit of the Lord (Acts 5.9).

In Acts 6.1, Luke reports a breakdown in fellowship. Those who sold property brought the money from the sale and laid it at the apostles' feet (Acts 4.35, 37; 5.2), who would then distribute it to the needy. In the context of continued growth in the number of disciples Luke reports: 'a complaint arose on the part of the Hellenistic [Jews] against the [native] Hebrews, because their widows were being overlooked in the daily serving of food' (6.1b). Two positive things result from this breakdown of fellowship: First, the apostles choose to 'devote themselves to prayer and to the ministry of the word, rather than serving tables' (Acts 6.2, 4); and secondly, seven men qualified by a good reputation and charismatic experience—full of the Holy Spirit and wisdom—are put in charge of this task.

Thirdly, the fledgling prophetic community continually devoted itself to the breaking of bread. In light of the last Passover meal, which Jesus transformed into a celebration of the meaning of his crucifixion (Lk. 22.7-23), the breaking of bread is not some general sharing of meals in fellowship, but it is the specific celebration of the crucifixion. Luke reports how the prophetic community practiced this: 'And day by day continuing with one mind in the temple, and breaking bread from house to house, they were taking their meals together with gladness and sincerity of heart' (Acts 2.46). In other words, parallel to the manner by which the Jews celebrated the Passover at the temple and then from house to house, they gathered as a community on the Temple Mount to praise God and pray (cf. Lk. 24.53; Acts 3.1) and then divided into smaller groups to celebrate the Lord's Supper in various private homes.[3]

Fourthly, the fledgling prophetic community also continually devoted itself to prayer. Beginning with the opening episodes of his infancy narrative Luke has shown prayer to be the environment in which God acts. For example, it is at the hour for the burning of incense, while the multitude who were gathered on the Temple Mount were in prayer, that an angel of the Lord appeared to Zacharias to announce to him that his

---

3. The Passover lamb was sacrificed at the Temple (*m. Pes.* 5.1-10). The Passover meal was then celebrated in the home of the resident or visiting worshiper (e.g. Mt. 26.17-19; Mk 14.12-16; Lk. 22.7-13).

wife, Elizabeth, would bear him a son (Lk. 1.8-17). Further, while Jesus
was praying when he was baptized 'heaven was opened and the Holy
Spirit descended upon him in bodily form like a dove' (Lk. 3.21b, 22).
As it was for Jesus, so it was for the disciples—the Spirit was poured
out upon them at a time when they were continually devoting themselves to prayer (Acts 1.14). Specifically, they were gathered on the
Temple Mount at the third hour, which is the hour of prayer, when the
Holy Spirit was poured out upon them. After the day of Pentecost, they
continued to gather together on the Temple Mount to pray (Acts 3.1;
4.31; 5.12). In these texts Luke reports that the disciples, whether a
group of 120 or of thousands, gathered together for corporate prayer on
the Temple Mount (as Israel also gathered for prayer).

Unity is a corollary of these four characteristics of the early prophetic
community—the apostles' teaching, fellowship, the breaking of bread
and prayer. As Luke reports this unity, the disciples day by day continue with one mind in the temple (Acts 2.46a). This echoes for the
larger community the unity which Luke had earlier reported for the 120
(Acts 1.14). In context it is having one mind, unity, about the apostles'
teaching, about sharing property and possessions, about celebrating the
Lord's Supper and about prayer—things which in the Church today are
all too often the causes of disunity. The unity continues, for example, in
the context of fellowship, or sharing property and possessions. Luke
reports: 'the congregation of those who believed were of one heart and
soul' (Acts 4.32a). Near the end of this period Luke reports they 'were
all with one accord in Solomon's portico' (Acts 5.12).

2.2. The Outer Life of the Community of Prophets

In his programmatic summary with which he introduces his narrative
about the acts of the prophetic community Luke not only introduces the
themes relating to the inner life of the community but he also introduces
the theme of the outer life of the community. This theme is witness.
This theme fulfills Jesus' post-resurrection promises to his disciples of
empowerment.

> You are witnesses of these things. And behold, I am sending forth the
> promise of My Father upon you; but you are to stay in the city until you
> are clothed with power from on high (Lk. 24.48-49).

> ...but you shall receive power when the Holy Spirit has come upon you;
> and you shall be My witnesses both in Jerusalem, and in all Judea and
> Samaria, and even to the remotest part of the earth (Acts 1.8).

As Luke reports it there are two complementary and interdependent aspects to this witness by the community of Spirit-baptized and empowered prophets. On the one hand, the disciples will witness by works of power. These works of power are the 'many signs and wonders [which] were taking place through the apostles' (Acts 2.43). On the other hand, the disciples will witness by words of power. These words of power are words inspired by the Spirit, such as, but not restricted to, the two pneuma discourses of Peter who witnessed when he was 'filled with the Holy Spirit' (Acts 2.4; 4.8). This witness of the disciples as a community of Spirit-baptized prophets echoes the pattern of the ministry of Jesus. In other words, just as it had been reported that Jesus was a 'prophet mighty/powerful in deed/work and word' (Lk. 24.19), so Luke reports that the disciples were a prophetic community powerful in works—signs and wonders—and powerful in words—prophetic speech.

2.2.1. *Witness by Works of Power.* Luke's report of the outer life of the community focuses on its witness by works of power. He reports: 'And every one kept feeling a sense of awe; and many wonders and signs were taking place through the apostles' (Acts 2.43). By this report Luke is not only announcing this as a theme for the acts of the prophetic community, but he is also reminding his readers that the disciples will continue Jesus' earlier ministry, because the same Spirit has been poured out upon them as had earlier empowered him. In the immediate context of this programmatic announcement that the apostles witnessed by means of signs and wonders, Peter has already spoken to the crowd on the Temple Mount about 'Jesus the Nazarene, a man attested to you by God with miracles, wonders and signs which God performed through Him in your midst' (Acts 2.22). As Peter summarizes it, the witness of Jesus, the anointed prophet was characterized by miracles, or acts of power, wonders and signs. Similarly the acts of power which God performed through the apostles, Spirit-baptized prophets, were characterized by wonders and signs.

One of the first miracles or acts of power which Jesus performed after the Spirit had anointed him was the healing of a paralyzed man (Lk. 5.17-26). Having returned to Galilee earlier in the power of the Spirit from his period of testing (Lk. 4.14), on this occasion, 'the power of the Lord was [present] for Him to perform healing' (Lk. 5.17). The lame man was healed, Jesus' critics were silenced, and the crowd which was gathered around were seized with astonishment. Similarly one of the

first miracles which the apostles performed after the Spirit had baptized
them was the healing of a lame man (Acts 3.1-11). Luke's report of this
miracle follows the structure of his Pentecost narrative which is: (1) sign
(Acts 2.1-4); (2) wonder (Acts 2.5-13); and (3) witness (Acts 2.4-36).
In Luke's report the sign is the healing of the lame man—in itself an act
of power (Acts 3.1-8). The wonder is the amazement which filled the
crowd when they saw what had happened to him (Acts 3.9-10). The
witness is Peter's preaching about Jesus as God's servant (Acts 3.11-
26). In fact, this narrative reports a witness to Jesus which is powerful
in work and word. Later the Sanhedrin will inquire of Peter and John
about this, asking: 'By what power, or in what name, have you done
this?' (Acts 4.7b). They also acknowledge that a noteworthy miracle-
sign had been performed (Acts 4.16). After Peter and John have been
released by the Sanhedrin they join the community in praying:

> grant that Thy bond-servants may speak Thy word with all confidence,
> while Thou dost extend Thy hand to heal, and signs and wonders take
> place through the name of Thy holy servant Jesus (Acts 4.29b-30).

In answer to this prayer, 'they were all filled with the Holy Spirit and
spoke the word of God with boldness' (Acts 4.31b). Further, 'with great
power the apostles were giving witness to the resurrection of the Lord
Jesus, and abundant grace was upon them all' (Acts 4.33).

The healing of the lame man is only one of the many wonders and
signs performed by the apostles and it is the only example described by
Luke. Nevertheless, Luke makes it clear that from first (Acts 2.43) to
last (Acts 5.12-16) that many acts of power were performed. Thus, he
reports once again: 'at the hands of the apostles many signs and wonders were taking place among the people' (Acts 5.12a). Both the sick
and those who were afflicted with demons were being healed (Acts
5.15-16). As a result of this witness by works of power, the people held
the disciples in high esteem (Acts 5.13), and multitudes of men and
women were added to the Church, that is, to the nation of Spirit-filled
prophets (Acts 4.31, 5.11).

2.2.2. *Witness by Words of Power*. In addition to, and complementing,
the witness by works of power, which echoes Jesus' own earlier ministry in power, the disciples as a prophetic community will also witness
by words of power. Luke reports this by giving specific examples of
inspired or prophetic speech. This is explicitly conveyed by the formula
'X was filled with the Holy Spirit', which Luke uses twice in this narra-

tive about the acts of the community of prophets.

The first use is in Luke's report of Peter's defense before the San-hedrin. He writes: 'Then Peter, filled with the Holy Spirit, said to them, "Rulers and elders of the people…" ' (Acts 4.8). This narrative echoes the Pentecost narrative in several essential features. Both have the introductory formula, 'filled with the Holy Spirit' (Acts 2.4, 4.8) which is followed by a report of direct speech, or pneuma discourse. This pneuma discourse, in fact, is a word of prophecy, for not only is this how Luke himself identifies the pneuma discourse in the case of Zach-ariah, but also he connects the introductory formula in the Pentecost narrative with the pneuma discourse by repeating the verb, αποφθέγ-γομαι for Peter's address to the crowd (Acts 2.4, 14). Thus, by echoing his Pentecost narrative in his report of Peter before the Sanhedrin, Luke portrays his defense to be a Spirit-inspired word of prophecy. Inci-dentally, this is the first recorded fulfillment of Jesus' promise of the Spirit's inspiration for when the disciples would be placed on trial (Lk. 12.11-12; 21.15). Luke uses the formula 'filled with the Holy Spirit' for the second time in his narrative about the acts of the community of prophets following the release of Peter and John by the Sanhedrin and the subsequent prayer meeting of the disciples. He reports: 'And when they had prayed the place where they had gathered together was shaken, and they were all filled with the Holy Spirit, and began to speak the words of God with boldness' (Acts 4.31). Luke adds the observation: 'And with great power the apostles were giving witness to the resur-rection' (Acts 4.33). As we have seen, Luke is here reporting a theo-phany on the Temple Mount, with an outburst of prophecy among all the disciples, numbered at 5000 men.

In his narrative about the acts of the community of prophets Luke reports three speeches: (1) Peter's speech following the healing of the lame man (Acts 3.11-26); (2) Peter's defense, or pneuma discourse before the Sanhedrin (Acts 4.8-12); and (3) the apostles' reply to the Sanhedrin (Acts 5.29-32). Comparing the first and third of these with the two pneuma discourses of Acts 2 and 4, one is justified in conclud-ing that, even though Luke has not introduced these speeches by the introductory formula 'filled with the Holy Spirit', they are also inspired by the Spirit. That is, they are also words of prophecy. I believe that, in fact, Luke intends his readers to understand that every witness by words of power in this narrative is prophecy. Clearly, not only was Jesus a prophet powerful in works and word, but the multitude of disciples in

Jerusalem following the pouring out of the Spirit in the day of Pentecost consists of prophets individually and corporately powerful in works and word.

To sum up, in post-Pentecost Jerusalem the people of God, initially a small company of prophets, rapidly grows to become the eschatological nation of prophets—the prophethood of all believers. In the events which Luke reports in his narrative of the acts of this prophetic community, Moses' earnest desire—'that all the Lord's people were prophets, that the Lord would put His Spirit upon them' (Num. 11.29)—is being fulfilled. Moreover, the implications of the nationwide pouring out of the Spirit which Joel announced (Joel 2.25-32) are being worked out in the acts of the prophetic community. Thus, this prophetic community, or nation of prophets, upon whom God has put His Spirit has an inner life characterized by: (1) the apostles' teaching; (2) fellowship; (3) the breaking of bread; and (4) prayer. Complementing this inner life, it has an outer life characterized by: (1) the witness by works of power; and (2) the witness by words of power. And so, in the advancing history of salvation, the acts of the community of prophets is a new eschatological reality in the era of the Spirit. No longer is the prophetic ministry limited to an individual, or to a select group, but it is now the reality for all of God's people—a veritable nation of prophets. Thus, in the weeks, months and early years following the pouring out of the Spirit of prophecy on the day of Pentecost the prophethood of all believers has been inaugurated.

Chapter 5

THE ACTS OF FIVE CHARISMATIC PROPHETS (ACTS 6.8–12.24)

Luke opened his second book, the Acts of the Apostles, with narratives which emphasized the disciples as a community or nation of prophets in terms of both their charismatic origins (Acts 1.6–2.41) and acts (Acts 2.42–6.7). However, Luke devotes about the last three-quarters of his narrative to reports about six leaders: Stephen, Philip, Barnabas, Agabus, Peter and Paul. Luke portrays each of these leaders to be a charismatic prophet. They typify the ministry of the prophethood of all believers, witnessing by works which were empowered by the Spirit and by words which were inspired by the Spirit.

Luke reports about these six charismatic leaders in pairs according to the office which they fill. Thus, of the seven deacons which the church in Jerusalem chose to supervise the daily distribution of food, Luke reports about two: Stephen and Philip. Similarly, from among the various groups of prophets, Luke reports about Barnabas and Agabus. Finally, from among the apostles, Luke reports primarily about Peter and Paul, the apostle to the Gentiles.[1] Whatever office or title Luke, or

1. It needs to be observed that contrary to Paul's own emphasis on his apostleship in his epistles Luke only identifies Paul as an apostle twice (Acts 14.4, 14), and then only in the same sense that his companion, Barnabas, is also an apostle. There are, perhaps, two reasons for Luke's determined refusal to identify Paul as an apostle. First, as a later convert to Christianity rather than being one of the original disciples, Paul does not meet the historical criterion for apostleship: 'beginning with the baptism of John, until the day that He was taken up from us' (Acts 1.22). Therefore, unlike Peter and the other apostles who were witnesses to the resurrection (Acts 1.22; 2.32; 3.15; 5.32, 10.39-41), he himself could not have been a witness to the resurrection. Secondly, throughout his narrative Luke's preferred category is 'prophet' rather than 'apostle', and, if he cannot portray Paul to be an apostle in the same sense that he portrays Peter to be an apostle, he does show Paul to be a prophet who is, in every particular, a prophet the equal of Peter (see Chapter 6 for a full exposition of the relevant data).

his modern interpreters, might assign to them, all function as charismatic prophets.[2] In Acts 1.8 Luke reports the mission of the disciples. They are to witness about Jesus by the power of the Spirit in Jerusalem, Judea and Samaria and to the ends of the earth. This is also programmatic for the structure of Luke's narrative. He reports the witness in Jerusalem in chs. 1–7, the witness in Samaria and (western) Judea in chs. 8–12 and the witness to the ends of the earth in chs. 13–28. Similarly, he reports about these six charismatic prophets on the same programmatic outline: Stephen witnessed in Jerusalem (Acts 6.8–7.60), Philip witnessed in Samaria (Acts 8.1-40), Peter witnessed in (western) Judea (Acts 9.32–12.24), and, finally, Paul witnessed to 'the ends of the earth' (12.25–28.31).

1. *The Acts of Stephen: A Charismatic Deacon (6.8–7.60)*

1.1. *Introduction: The Prophetic Community Chooses Seven Deacons*
Along with continually devoting themselves to the apostles' teaching, to the breaking of bread and to prayer, the community of Spirit-baptized prophets also continually devoted themselves to fellowship (Acts 2.42). In time, this fellowship within the community is broken or disturbed by two problems. First, it is disturbed by the dishonesty of Ananias and Sapphira in regards to the sale price of a piece of property (5.1-11). Secondly, it is broken some time later when 'a complaint arose on the part of the Hellenistic [Jews] against the [native] Hebrews, because their widows were being overlooked in the daily serving of food' (Acts 5.1b). The multitude of disciples solves the breakdown in the equitable distribution of food by choosing seven men, 'deacons',[3] to supervise the

2.   Whether the interpreter turns to commentaries, Bible dictionaries, theological wordbooks, etc., few standard study tools adequately communicate Luke's charismatic and prophetic perspectives to their readers. Hans Conzelmann, *The Acts of the Apostles* (trans. James Limburg, A. Thomas Kraabel and Donald H. Juel; Hermeneia; Philadelphia: Fortress Press, 1987) is an extreme example of this. Without too much exaggeration the reader of this commentary might complain: 'we have not even heard whether there is a Holy Spirit'. This typical neglect of Luke's charismatic theology indicates that the agenda and the theology of the interpreters are all too often out of step with Luke's agenda and theology.

3.   Of course, Luke does not actually use the Greek equivalent of the English word 'deacon'. Nevertheless, since the function of the seven is to 'serve tables' (διακονεῖν τραπεζαις) 'deacon' is a better title for this office than other titles, such as 'almoner' (for this term see F.F. Bruce, *Peter, Stephen, James and John: Studies*

distribution. These seven deacons were chosen on the basis of two qualifications. First, they were to be men of good reputation, which in the context of 'fellowship' would relate specifically to their ability to administrate the money which many disciples had been bringing to the apostles (Acts 2.45; 4.34, 35, 37; 5.1, 2). Secondly, they were to be men who were also full of the Holy Spirit and wisdom (Acts 6.3). This second qualification, namely, that they were to be full of the Holy Spirit, makes these men to be charismatic deacons rather than just good business administrators. In order to illustrate the ministries of these seven charismatic administrators, Luke reports about two of them: Stephen (Acts 6.8–7.60) and Philip (Acts 8.1-40).

1.2. *Stephen: A Charismatic Deacon*[4]

Stephen is the first of the charismatic leaders about whom Luke reports. Luke describes his charismatic life and ministry using a variety of terms. For example, as one of the seven Stephen was 'full of the Holy Spirit and wisdom' (Acts 6.3). When Luke subsequently names him as one of the seven whom the multitude chose he describes him as

in Early Non-Pauline Christianity [Grand Rapids: Eerdmans, 1980], p. 51). If the seven are not to be identified as 'deacons' then they should be identified as 'table servers' (though this term has the disadvantage of connoting 'waiters' rather than 'administrators').

4. Luke's report about Stephen is a typical example of how the agenda and/or the theology of interpreters are out of step with Luke's agenda and theology. In his brief report about Stephen, Luke gives four direct and one indirect references to his experience of the Spirit—the highest concentration of references to a person's experience of the Spirit in Luke–Acts apart from Luke's report about Jesus' experience of the Spirit. Yet in his chapter 'Stephen and the Hellenists' in *Peter, Stephen, James and John*, p. 59, F.F. Bruce simply comments: 'Luke, at any rate, looks on all seven as Spirit-filled men, Stephen outstandingly so (Acts 6.3, 5).' Similarly, Graham Stanton, 'Stephen in Lucan Perspective', in E.A. Livingstone (eds.), *Studia Biblica 1978. III. Papers on Paul and Other New Testament Authors* (JSNTSup, 3; Sheffield: JSOT Press, 1980), p. 355, makes but one comment on Stephen's experience of the Spirit: 'Stephen's accusers oppose the Holy Spirit, but in stark contrast Stephen himself, full of the Holy Spirit, gazes into heaven and sees the glory of God and Jesus standing at the right hand of God (v. 55).' Nowhere do these interpreters show any awareness that Luke portrays Stephen as a disciple whose works were empowered by the Spirit and whose words, that is, his reply to the High Priest's question, were inspired by the Spirit. This neglect of a subject which is so prominent in Luke's narrative is deplorable. The other leaders, who are the subjects of this chapter, suffer similarly at the hands of many interpreters.

'a man full of faith and of the Holy Spirit' (Acts 6.5). Further, Stephen 'was performing great wonders and signs among the people' because he was 'full of grace and power' (Acts 6.8). In addition, Luke reports how some men from the Synagogue of the Freedmen were 'unable to cope with the wisdom and the Spirit with which he was speaking' (Acts 6.10). Finally, Luke describes Stephen as having a vision of the exalted Lord Jesus moments before his martyrdom when he was 'full of the Holy Spirit' (Acts 7.55).

Luke's fivefold description of this charismatic dimension of Stephen's life and ministry is unparalleled in Acts. Indeed, apart from his description of Jesus (Lk. 3–4) no one else in the New Testament is described by such a concentration of references to the Holy Spirit. On the one hand, then, Luke understands Stephen to be a typical representative of the ministries of these seven deacons. On the other hand, Luke understands Stephen to be a charismatic deacon par excellence, unequaled among the apostles and other disciples in his experience of the Spirit. Because of his experience of the Spirit, Stephen, Luke reports, witnessed both by works which were empowered by the Spirit and by words which were inspired by the Spirit.

1.3. *The Acts of Stephen*
Like the charismatic ministries of Jesus, the Spirit-anointed prophet, and of the disciples, the Spirit-baptized prophets, which Luke has reported earlier, the acts of this charismatic deacon Stephen are also of two complementary kinds: (1) acts of power (Acts 6.8-9); and (2) Spirit-inspired speech. Luke's description of the seven deacons as men full of the Holy Spirit and wisdom (Acts 6.3) is programmatic for Stephen's twofold ministry. In other words, the description 'full of the Holy Spirit' is programmatic for the acts of power which Stephen performed (Acts 6.8-9), and the term 'full...of wisdom' is programmatic for the Spirit-inspired witness with which Stephen was speaking (Acts 6.10). Like his charismatic predecessors and his charismatic contemporaries, Stephen was a man (a prophet) powerful in works and word.

1.3.1. *Stephen Performed Great Wonders and Signs*. As we have already observed Luke describes Stephen's charismatic ministry as 'full of grace and power' (Acts 6.8a). This gives further definition to Stephen as the man who is 'full of the Spirit' (Acts 6.3) and described as 'full of faith and the Holy Spirit' (Acts 6.5), a description where 'faith' likely means miracle-working faith. The result of Stephen being

'full of grace and power' was that he performed unspecified 'great wonders and signs' (Acts 6.8b). This threefold description of Stephen (power, wonders and signs) echoes Peter's earlier witness about Jesus who was attested to the Jews by God 'with miracles [i.e. works of power] and wonders and signs' (Acts 2.22). Similarly, Luke has also reported that subsequently to the pouring out of the Spirit in power for witness on the day of Pentecost the apostles performed many wonders and signs (Acts 2.43). Further, toward the end of his narrative on the acts of the community of prophets, Luke reported that 'at the hands of the apostles many signs and wonders were taking place among the people' (Acts 5.12). Two significant conclusions for Luke's report about Stephen's charismatic ministry follow from his earlier reports about Jesus and the apostles: (1) since the threefold description, power, wonders and signs describes miracles of healing for the acts of Jesus and the apostles, then it must also describe unidentified miracles of healing for the acts of Stephen; and (2) Luke's report about Stephen (and, next, of Philip) shows that these acts of power, wonders and signs are not exclusive to the apostles, but are performed by other disciples as well.

Luke describes these miracles of healing power which Stephen performed as 'great' (μεγάλα) wonders and signs. In other words, at a time when it was commonplace for 'many' wonders and signs to be performed by the apostles (Acts 2.43; 5.12) Stephen's miracles of healing stood out as 'great' or very notable. In addition, these wonders and signs which Stephen performed were multiple, not just one or two. In other words, even though Luke does not report any examples of them, they were as characteristic or typical of his ministry as they were characteristic of the acts of the apostles. Thus, like the charismatic prophets who preceded him, namely, Jesus (Acts 2.22) and the apostles (Acts 2.43), Stephen witnessed by works which were empowered by the Spirit.

1.3.2. *Stephen Witnessed with the Spirit's Wisdom.* Complementing Stephen's witness by works which were empowered by the Spirit was his witness by words inspired by the Spirit. The multitude of disciples in Jerusalem choose Stephen to be one of the seven because he was both 'full of the Spirit and of wisdom' (Acts 6.3). Further, those men from the Synagogue of the Freedman to whom Stephen witnessed, 'were unable to cope with the wisdom and the Spirit with which he was speaking' (Acts 6.10). Stephen's experience with these men from the synagogue directly fulfills Jesus' earlier promise to the disciples, namely, 'I will give you utterance and wisdom which none of your opponents will be able to resist or refute' (Lk. 21.15).

In the context of Luke's narrative Stephen's defense before the Council or Sanhedrin (Acts 7.2-53), the importance of which is indicated by the fact that it is the longest speech in Acts, is a wisdom saying. However, since the wisdom which Jesus would give to defend his disciples when they were put on trial is linked to the giving of the Spirit (Lk. 12.13; Acts 6.10) this wisdom saying is also to be classified as a pneuma discourse. That is, like Peter's earlier defense before this same Council (Acts 4.8-12), it is prophetic speech inspired by the Spirit. Luke emphasizes the supernatural Spirit-inspired character of Stephen's defense before the Sanhedrin by his typical strategy of inclusio. That defense is prefaced by the twofold description Stephen as 'full of the Spirit and of wisdom' (Acts 6.3) and as 'full of faith and of the Holy Spirit' (Acts 6.5). It is concluded by the report that Stephen was 'full of the Holy Spirit' (Acts 7.55). Clearly, Stephen's defense before the Sanhedrin in its entirety is inspired by the Holy Spirit and is, therefore, a prophetic denunciation of the leaders of the nation of Israel.

As Luke reports it, when Stephen makes his defense before the Sanhedrin, he is conscious of his role as a Spirit-inspired prophet. When he accuses the Council's members of 'always resisting the Holy Spirit', he is accusing them of now resisting his own Spirit-ful defense (he is 'full of the Holy Spirit', Acts 7.55), just as, for example, they had earlier resisted the Spirit-filled defense of Peter (Acts 4.8-22). This 'stiff-necked and uncircumcised in heart' resisting of the Holy Spirit continues and climaxes the ongoing history of their fathers who persecuted the prophets (Acts 7.52a). In other words, just as, according to Stephen, their fathers killed the prophets who announced the Righteous One, they have betrayed and murdered the Righteous One (Acts 7.52b). The Sanhedrin fully recognizes the implications of Stephen's accusations, and just as Jesus died in Jerusalem as a rejected prophet, though he was powerful in works and word (Lk. 13.33-35; 24.19, 20), so Stephen will also die in Jerusalem as a rejected prophet, though he too was powerful in works and word (Acts 6.8, 10)—like Jesus before him, wrongly suffering the penalty due to a false prophet (Deut. 18.20).[5]

---

5.   See p. 102 below for a survey of the parallels between Jesus and Stephen.

2. *The Acts of Philip: A Charismatic Deacon (8.1-40)*

2.1. *Introduction*

In his narrative about the acts of these six charismatic prophets Luke, as we have observed, reports these leaders in three pairs. Philip is the second of the charismatic deacons whose ministry he reports. Stephen has a prophetic ministry in Jerusalem; Philip has a prophetic ministry in Samaria. Like Stephen, Philip is first introduced into the narrative as being one of the seven men who were put in charge of the daily serving of food to the needy widows of the church in Jerusalem. Therefore, he is also a man 'of good reputation, full of the Holy Spirit and wisdom' (Acts 6.3). Thus, he is not only a good administrator, but he is also a charismatic deacon. Later, Luke will inform his readers that in addition to his role as a deacon Philip also does the work of an evangelist (Acts 21.8).

2.2. *Philip: A Charismatic Deacon*

Luke reports Philip's experience of the Holy Spirit in three texts. First, as we have already seen, along with Stephen and the other five, he is 'full of the Holy Spirit and wisdom' (Acts 6.3). As such, Philip both performed signs and great miracles, such as casting out demons and healing the sick (Acts 8.6, 7, 13), and preached the good news about the kingdom of God (Acts 8.12). Thus, like Jesus, the apostles and Stephen, Philip was a man who was also powerful in works and word. Secondly, the Spirit spoke to Philip, directing him to go up and join the chariot of the Ethiopian court official who was returning to Ethiopia after worshiping in Jerusalem (Acts 8.29). Thirdly, after Philip had baptized this Ethiopian court official, 'the Spirit of the Lord snatched Philip away' (Acts 8.39; cf. 1 Kgs 18.12; Ezek. 3.12, 14), miraculously transporting him to Azotus. Philip's threefold experience of the Spirit—(1) being 'full of the Holy Spirit', resulting in a Spirit-empowered witness by works and by word; (2) the leading of the Spirit; and (3) being miraculously transported by the Spirit from one location to another—makes him more than just a charismatic deacon. These experiences of the Spirit make him a prophet. Incidentally, not only is he a prophet himself, but his four unmarried daughters will later be prophetesses (Acts 21.9).

2.3. *The Acts of Philip in Samaria (8.4-13)*

Luke introduces his narrative about Philip by reporting that following the death of Stephen, 'a great persecution arose against the church in

Jerusalem' (Acts 8.2a). As a result the disciples were 'scattered throughout the regions of Judea and Samaria' (Acts 8.2b). Further, Luke reports, 'those who had been scattered went about preaching the word' (Acts 8.4). As one of those who had been scattered, 'Philip went down to the city of Samaria and [began] proclaiming Christ to them' (Acts 8.5). Just as the earlier ministries of Jesus (Acts 2.22), the apostles (Acts 2.43; 5.12) and Stephen (Acts 6.8) had been attested by wonders and signs, so Philip's witness that Jesus was the Christ, or Messiah, was also attested by signs (Acts 8.6), namely, the casting out of unclean spirits and healing of many who had been paralyzed and lame (Acts 8.7). In the context of Luke's description of Simon the magician, Luke identifies these signs as 'great miracles' or great acts of power (Acts 8.13). This twofold pattern of Philip's signs—casting out demons and healing the sick—echoes the pattern of Jesus' own Spirit-anointed prophetic ministry, when he began his ministry 'in the power of the Spirit' (Lk. 4.14), and, subsequently cast out demons (Lk. 4.33-37) and healed the sick (Lk. 4.38, 39). Though Jesus is the Christ, or Messiah, and Philip is one of the seven, Philip can minister with the same power as Jesus, the Messiah whom he proclaims, because both are 'full of the Holy Spirit' (Lk. 4.1; Acts 6.3). The result of this witness by works of power was that 'there was much rejoicing in the city' (Acts 8.8), 'they believed...[and] were being baptized' (Acts 8.12) and 'Samaria had received the word of God' (Acts 8.14).

2.4. *Philip Witnesses to an Ethiopian (8.26-40)*
After Philip had witnessed in Samaria by performing signs, or works of power (Acts 8.4-25), the Lord directed him to witness by words of power (Acts 8.26-40). Earlier the Lord had directed Philip to Samaria providentially, because of persecution against the church in Jerusalem (Acts 8.1-4). At this point the Lord leads Philip directly. Luke reports how 'an angel of the Lord spoke to Philip saying, "arise and go south..."' (Acts 8.26), and, further, that 'the Spirit said to Philip, "go up and join this chariot"' (Acts 8.29). Having obeyed this leading of the Spirit, Philip discussed a scripture from the prophet Isaiah with him, and 'beginning from this scripture he preached Jesus to him' (Acts 8.36). The Ethiopian court official believed Philip's witness about Jesus and was baptized (Acts 8.38). Luke then reports: 'and when they came up out of the water, the Spirit of the Lord snatched Philip away; and the eunuch saw him no more, but went on his way rejoicing' (Acts 8.39).

Philip's witness to this Ethiopian court official was effective because, like Stephen's witness in Jerusalem, it was inspired by the Spirit. This is confirmed by two observations. First, like Stephen, Philip is not only full of the Holy Spirit but also of that 'wisdom' which comes from the Spirit (Acts 6.3); and secondly, Philip's witness to the Ethiopian is both introduced and concluded by references to the Holy Spirit, on the narrative strategy of inclusio (Acts 8.29, 39). Thus, Luke's report about Philip's twofold ministry, first in Samaria, and secondly, to the Ethiopian court official, shows that on the one hand, he witnessed by works which were empowered by the Spirit, and on the other hand, he witnessed by words of wisdom which were inspired by the Spirit. In other words, Philip is another example of the many disciples who were prophets powerful in works and word.

3. The Acts of Barnabas: A Charismatic Prophet

3.1. Introduction

Like the apostles and the many other members of the charismatic community, both Stephen and Philip were prophets. Luke, however, has not identified them as such. This identification must be inferred from his report of their experience of the Spirit and his report of their twofold witness by works which were empowered by the Spirit and words which were inspired by the Spirit. In contrast to his reports about Stephen and Philip, Luke explicitly identifies Barnabas, the third charismatic leader about whom he reports, as a charismatic prophet (Acts 13.1).

Luke introduces Barnabas into his narrative about the acts of the prophetic community as a positive example of 'fellowship' (Acts 4.34-37), in contrast to Ananias and Sapphira who were negative examples of fellowship (Acts 5.1-11). When Luke introduces Barnabas he identifies him as 'Joseph, a Levite of Cyprian birth, who was also called Barnabas' (Acts 4.36). Luke tells his readers that when Barnabas is translated into Greek it means 'Son of Encouragement' (υἱὸς παρα-κλήσεως). Since Luke later reports that Barnabas does the hortatory work which is characteristic of the prophet (Acts 11.23, παρακλειν; cf. Acts 14.22; 15.32), and since he also identifies Barnabas as a prophet (Acts 13.1), the name 'Son of Encouragement' identifies Barnabas as a prophet and may, therefore, be translated into English as 'Son of prophecy'.[6] Barnabas reappears in narratives which encompass a time span of about 15 years: first, acting as a champion of the newly converted Saul (Acts 9.26-30); secondly, as the representative of the Jerusalem church in Antioch (Acts 11.22-30); thirdly as one of five prophets and teachers in the church at Antioch (Acts 13.1-3); and fourthly, as the companion of Paul on his first evangelistic tour (Acts 13.4–15.35). Finally, Barnabas disappears from Luke's narrative when he and Paul have a sharp disagreement about taking John, called Mark, along with them on their second evangelistic tour (Acts 15.36-41). Because of this disagreement, 'Barnabas took Mark with him and sailed away to Cyprus' (Acts 15.39b).

3.2. *Barnabas: A Charismatic Prophet*

Luke reports several dimensions of Barnabas' ministry as a charismatic prophet. For example, he reports that, like Stephen (Acts 6.5), Barnabas was 'full of the Holy Spirit and of faith' (Acts 11.24). Further, like the apostles as prophets, he also had a teaching ministry (Acts 11.26; cf. 2.42). Moreover, along with Simeon, Lucius, Manaen and Saul, Barnabas is one of the 'prophets and teachers' in the church that was at Antioch. In addition, along with some other disciples he was 'continually filled with joy and with the Holy Spirit' (Acts 13.52). Finally, like all of the charismatic prophets who preceded him, Barnabas, in company with Paul, is a prophet who was powerful in works and word. Thus, at Pisidian Antioch he spoke out boldly (Acts 13.46; cf. 4.13, 31), and at Iconium he performed signs and wonders (Acts 14.3; cf. 2.43; 5.12; 6.8; 8.6, 13). Clearly, he also witnessed by works which were empowered by the Spirit and by words which were inspired by the Spirit.

4. *The Acts of Agabus: A Charismatic Prophet*

Luke introduces Agabus into his narrative when he is reporting Barnabas' ministry at Antioch (Acts 11.22-30). He reports that after Barnabas had brought Saul to Antioch from Tarsus (Acts 11.25, 26), 'some prophets came down from Jerusalem to Antioch' (Acts 11.27). One of this company of prophets from Jerusalem was named Agabus (Acts 11.28a). Luke reports how he 'indicated by the Spirit that there would

---

6.   E. Earle Ellis, *Prophecy and Hermeneutic in Early Christianity* (Grand Rapids: Eerdmans, 1978), p. 131.

certainly be a great famine all over the world' (Acts 11.28b). The practical outcome of this prophecy was that the disciples at Antioch sent a contribution for famine relief to the elders at Jerusalem in charge of Barnabas and Saul (Acts 11.29, 30).

At this point, shortly before the first evangelistic tour, Agabus disappears from Luke's narrative until that time when Luke reports about Paul's final journey to Jerusalem at the end of his third evangelistic tour. When Paul arrived at Tyre, the disciples there 'kept telling Paul through the Spirit not to set foot in Jerusalem' (Acts 21.4). When Paul arrived at Caesarea, Luke adds, 'a certain prophet named Agabus came down from Judea' (Acts 21.10). Agabus took 'Paul's belt and bound his own feet and hands' (Acts 21.11a). Adding voice to action he then said, 'this is what the Holy Spirit says: "In this way the Jews at Jerusalem will bind the man who owns this belt and deliver him into the hands of the Gentiles"' (Acts 21.11b). In each of his two appearances in Luke's narrative, Agabus qualifies as a prophet because he speaks words which are inspired by the Spirit.

5. *The Acts of Peter: A Charismatic Apostle*

5.1. *Introduction*

Peter is prominent in both the Gospels and the Acts. He was one of the first disciples (Lk. 5.1-11) and, along with James and John, he was one of the inner circle of disciples (Lk. 8.51). Peter was spiritually perceptive and was the first disciple to recognize that Jesus was the Messiah (Lk. 9.20). Sometimes, as when he was on the Mount of Transfiguration, he also spoke without realizing what he was saying (Lk. 9.33). In spite of all his good qualities Peter would deny Jesus three times (Lk. 22.34, 54-62). The Peter of Acts is different from the Peter of the Gospels in that the glaring weaknesses of the gospel period are no longer evident in Acts. The primary basis for the change between the Peter of the Gospels and the Peter of the Acts is his reception of the Holy Spirit on the day of Pentecost.

As Luke's narrative of the acts of the six charismatic prophets unfolds the programmatic outline for the geographic spread of the Spirit-empowered witness continues to be fulfilled. Stephen gave his Spirit-empowered witness in Jerusalem. Philip gave his Spirit-empowered witness in Samaria, and Peter gives his Spirit-empowered witness in Judea (Acts 9.32–10.48).

5.2. *Peter: A Charismatic Apostle*

In the earlier discussion of the origin of the prophetic community (Acts 1.6–2.41) and the acts of the prophetic community (Acts 2.42–6.7) we have examined Peter's ministry as a charismatic apostle. At this point, therefore, we need only briefly recapitulate what has already been discussed. Peter's experience of the Spirit began on the day of Pentecost when he, along with his fellow disciples, was 'filled with the Holy Spirit and began to speak with other tongues as the Spirit gave utterance' (Acts 2.4). The formula 'filled with the Holy Spirit' and the prophecy from Joel which this experience fulfills both mean that Peter has received the Spirit of prophecy. This pouring out of the Spirit of prophecy upon Peter and his fellow disciples means that, on the one hand, he will witness about Jesus by works which will be empowered by the Spirit, and, on the other hand, he will witness by words which will be inspired by the Spirit. Indeed, everything which Luke reports about Peter from his reception of the Spirit on the day of Pentecost until he disappears from the narrative following the Jerusalem Council is consistent with this identification of the apostle Peter as a prophet who was powerful in works and word.

5.3. *The Acts of Peter*

Luke portrays the Peter of Acts as a charismatic apostle and prophet from first to last. He not only ministered as a charismatic apostle and prophet in Jerusalem (Acts 2.14-41), but also in Samaria (Acts 8.14-25) and in western Judea (Acts 9.32–10.48).

5.3.1. *The Acts of Peter in Jerusalem (2.14–6.7)*. Luke's report about the origin of the prophetic community (Acts 1.6–2.41) and also of the acts of the prophetic community (Acts 2.42–6.7), in contrast to his report about the six charismatic prophets (Acts 6.8–28.31), focuses upon the ministry of the disciples as a community. Nevertheless, in spite of Luke's emphasis on the disciples as a prophetic community, Peter is the dominant disciple in these two narratives. As we have seen Peter witnessed by words which were inspired by the Spirit. For example, both his Pentecost address (Acts 2.14-39) and his defense before the Sanhedrin (Acts 4.8-12) are pneuma discourses, that is, prophetic speeches which were inspired by the Spirit. By analogy with these two pneuma discourses both his witness after the healing of the lame man (Acts 3.12-26) and his second defense before the Sanhedrin

(Acts 5.29-32) are also prophetic speech inspired by the Spirit (note especially Acts 5.32).

Not only did Peter witness in Jerusalem by words which were inspired by the Spirit, but he also witnessed in Jerusalem by works which were empowered by the Spirit. For example, he was one of the apostles through whom many signs and wonders were taking place after the pouring out of the Spirit on the day of Pentecost (Acts 2.43). The healing of the lame man by Peter was a notable example of these early wonders and signs (3.1-10). Wonders and signs continued to characterize the Spirit-empowered witness of the apostles (Acts 4.29-33; 5.12). The remarkable power of Peter's shadow to heal the sick who were laid on cots and pallets in the streets of Jerusalem is a later notable example of the apostles' witness in Jerusalem by works which were empowered by the Spirit.

5.3.2. The Acts of Peter in Samaria (8.14-25). Because of the persecution which broke out against the disciples in Jerusalem following the death of Stephen (Acts 8.1-14), Philip, one of the seven charismatic deacons, went down to Samaria. There, as we have seen, he witnessed about Jesus by both works and words which were empowered by the Spirit. The result of this witness was that many believed and were baptized (Acts 8.12). When the apostles in Jerusalem learned of Philip's success they sent both Peter and John down to Samaria (Acts 8.14-25). Peter had a threefold ministry in Samaria. First, along with John, Peter prayed that these Samaritan believers would receive the Holy Spirit (Acts 8.15-17, cf. Lk. 11.13). This prayer was answered as Simon the magician's response confirmed (Acts 8.18, 19). Secondly, Peter cursed this same Simon because he had thought that he could obtain the gift of God with money (Acts 8.20). Thirdly, Peter (and John) preached the gospel to many of the villages of the Samaritans while they were en route back to Jerusalem. This report about Peter's threefold ministry in Samaria has only one reference to the Holy Spirit, namely, the Spirit was bestowed through the laying on of Peter's hands. This one reference, however, is Luke's reminder to his readers that Peter continues to minister as a charismatic apostle and prophet.

5.3.3. The Acts of Peter in Judea (9.32–10.48). In his first book Luke reported how Jesus had an itinerant or peripatetic ministry, not only throughout Galilee and Judea, but even in the Gentile territories of

Sidon and Decapolis. Like Jesus, Peter also has an itinerant or peri-patetic ministry. In fact, he is the first of the disciples whom Luke reports to have had a peripatetic ministry (Acts 9.32). During his walk-about witness Peter goes to Lydda (Acts 9.32), Joppa (Acts 9.36) and Caesarea (Acts 10.1, 24) before returning to Jerusalem (Acts 11.2). During his walkabout through western Judea, Peter witnesses by works empowered by the Spirit and also by words inspired by the Spirit.

Luke reports that Peter performed signs and wonders in western Judea just as he had earlier performed signs and wonders in Jerusalem. For example, in Lydda he healed a lame man (Acts 9.32-35) just as he had earlier healed the lame man at the Beautiful Gate in Jerusalem (Acts 3.1-10). As a result of this act of power many at Lydda and Sharon turned to the Lord (Acts 9.35). In addition, at Joppa Peter raised a certain disciple, named Tabitha or Dorcas, from the dead (Acts 9.40), a mighty act which is uniquely associated with charismatic prophets such as Elijah and Elisha (1 Kgs 17.17-24; 2 Kgs 4.29-37) and Jesus (Lk. 7.14-16). As a result of this mighty miracle many in Joppa believed in the Lord (Acts 9.42).

Luke also reports that Peter witnessed to Cornelius and his household in Caesarea. Luke does not, however, preface Peter's witness in word by the 'filled with the Holy Spirit' formula which introduces a pneuma discourse or by prophetic speech inspired by the Spirit. Nevertheless, it is implied. On the one hand, Peter is led to go to this Gentile household by the combination of a preparatory vision (Acts 10.9-16), which in both the Old and New Testaments is a medium of prophetic revelation (Num. 12.6; Acts 2.17), and by direct instruction from the Spirit (Acts 10.19, 20). On the other hand, the pouring out of the Spirit which com-plements Peter's witness (Acts 10.44-48) is a baptizing with the Spirit such as Peter and the other disciples had themselves experienced on the day of Pentecost (Acts 11.15-17). In light of Luke's overall emphasis on Spirit-inspired words of witness throughout his narrative, and, in this narrative, both the leading of the Spirit and the gift of the Spirit, it is inconceivable that Peter witnessed to Cornelius by anything less than words which were inspired by the Spirit.

As Luke has reported, Peter's peripatetic ministry through western Judea as apostle and prophet echoed Jesus' peripatetic ministry. His ministry was Christ-like in that he healed the lame, raised the dead and had an itinerant ministry that included the Gentiles. Further, Luke reports how Peter personally fulfilled the programmatic outline of witness reported at the beginning of Acts (Acts 1.8). In geographical terms he ministered in Jerusalem, then in Samaria and, finally, in Judea. In racial terms he ministered to Jews and Samaritans and his visit to Cornelius establishes the precedent for ministry to Gentiles. In other words, Peter was a prophet who was powerful in works and word in Jerusalem, in Samaria and in Judea; that is, powerful in works and word to the Jews, to the Samaritans and to the Gentiles. In light of this record it is little wonder that Peter is so prominent in Luke's report of the origin of the prophetic community (Acts 1.12–2.41), the acts of the prophetic community (Acts 2.42–6.7) and the acts of six charismatic prophets (Acts 6.8–28.31). It is little wonder, further, that Peter's experience of the Spirit and his prophetic ministry provide the standard by which Luke measures Paul's experience of the Spirit and his prophetic ministry. Indeed, as much as, or more than Paul, Peter is Luke's great hero of the prophetic community in action.

To sum up, my survey of Luke's narrative about the acts of these five charismatic prophets (Acts 6.8–12.24) has consistently shown that their ministries consist of works which are empowered by the Spirit and words which are inspired by the Spirit. Luke gives no other picture in this narrative or, indeed, earlier in Acts or in his first account about Jesus who was a prophet mighty in works and word (Lk. 24.19). Not only so, but these charismatic prophets simply represent and illustrate the reality of the prophethood of all believers. Thus, for example, in Luke's narrative, Stephen and Philip are not the only charismatic deacons—the other five are charismatic deacons too (Acts 6.3). Similarly, Barnabas and Agabus are not the only prophets. Each represents a group of prophets (Acts 11.27; 13.1). Finally, Peter is not the only charismatic apostle. The other eleven are also charismatic apostles (Acts 2.4). Indeed, not only are these leaders all charismatic prophets in function, but, beginning with the pouring out of the Spirit on the day of Pentecost, all of the disciples are charismatic prophets (Acts 2.4; 4.31). This is equally as true of Samaritan believers and Gentile converts (Acts 8.15-17; 10.44-48) as it is of the disciples in Jerusalem. Thus, the disciples generally exemplify the prophethood of all believers. As Luke also shows, their leaders, represented in Luke's narrative by Stephen, Philip, Barnabas, Agabus and Peter, could be no less. It now remains for Luke to show that the convert, Saul of Tarsus, like Peter and the others before him, is also a charismatic prophet (Acts 12.25–28.31).

6. Parallels between Jesus and Stephen

Luke has portrayed Stephen as a charismatic deacon and prophet par excellence—from first to last 'full of the Holy Spirit' (Acts 6.3; 7.55). In addition, Stephen is a unique Christ-like figure in the New Testament. The following chart illustrates the amazing points of correspondence between these two men of the Spirit:

Jesus (Luke)	*Stephen (Acts)*
full of the Holy Spirit 4.1	full of the Holy Spirit 6.3; 6.5; 7.55
he kept increasing in wisdom 2.52	full of wisdom 6.3, 10
Jesus returned to Galilee in the power of the Spirit 4.14	full of grace and power 6.8
miracles and wonders and signs which God performed through him Acts 2.22	performed great wonders and signs 6.8
accused of blasphemy 5.21	accused of blasphemy 6.11
rejected by elders, chief priests and scribes 9.22; 22.66	opposed by scribes and elders 6.12 false witnesses speak against him 6.13
speaks against Jerusalem and temple 19.41-46; 21.6	speaks against temple 6.13; 7.46-50
his face became different and his clothing white and gleaming 9.29	had the (white/radiant) face of an angel 6.15 (cf. Lk. 24.4)
rejection of the prophets motif 4.24-30	rejection of the prophets motif 7.51-53
trial: refers to heavenly Son of man 22.69	trial: refers to the heavenly Son of man 7.56
crucified, cries out: 'Father, into Thy hands I commit my Spirit' 23.46a	dying, prays: 'Lord Jesus, receive my Spirit' 7.59
crucified, prays: 'Father, forgive them for they do not know what they are doing' 23.34	dying, prays: 'Lord, do not hold this sin against them' 7.60a
crucified: he breathed his last 23.46b	martyred: he fell asleep 7.60b

These parallels between Jesus, the charismatic Christ, and Stephen, the charismatic deacon, are like the earlier parallels between Elijah and Elisha, who both ministered to Gentiles, multiplied food, raised the dead, parted the Jordan, and so on, but are more extended and are, if possible, of a higher order. The full significance of these parallels between Jesus and Stephen must forever remain locked in Luke's mind alone. The reader, however, can infer that their significance relates to their unique position in the unfolding of salvation history. It is through

Jesus' ministry and death as the rejected prophet that the provision of salvation is made; it is through Stephen's ministry and death as a rejected prophet that Christianity begins its decisive break with Judaism and salvation begins to be taken to the Samaritans and ultimately to the Gentiles.

Chapter 6

THE ACTS OF PAUL: A CHARISMATIC PROPHET
(ACTS 12.25–28.31)

In the final section of his book 'The Acts of the Apostles', Luke discusses six charismatic prophets in pairs: two charismatic deacons (Stephen, Philip), two charismatic prophets (Barnabas, Agabus) and two charismatic apostles (Peter, Paul). Based on this narrative strategy Paul should have been paired with Peter in Chapter 5. Luke's report about Paul, however, spanning as it does approximately 15 years of activity, and extending from chs. 13–28, requires its own chapter.

Luke introduces Paul in his narrative at the stoning of Stephen. In this episode, the witnesses of Stephen's stoning, 'laid aside their robes at the feet of a young man named Saul' (Acts 7.58). Though Luke first introduces Saul/Paul as a participant in the execution of Stephen as a false prophet, he later reports some biographical information about Paul. He was born in Tarsus of Cilicia, but brought up in Jerusalem, perhaps by his sister (Acts 22.3, 16). As a son of Pharisees he was educated as a Pharisee by the great rabbi, Gamaliel (Acts 22.3; 23.6). He was also, somewhat unexpectedly, a Roman citizen by birth (Acts 16.37; 22.25-28).

Though he had been educated by Gamaliel, Saul, the pupil, was of a different temperament than his master. Earlier, when the apostles were on trial before the Sanhedrin, Gamaliel had counselled the Sanhedrin to adopt a 'hands-off' policy (Acts 5.34-40), but Stephen's execution catapults Paul from an approving spectator to a zealous persecutor. Luke reports that 'Saul began ravaging the church' (Acts 8.3a) like a savage wolf among a flock of sheep. He did this by 'entering house after house; and dragging off men and women, he put them in prison' (Acts 8.3b). His appetite apparently unsatiated by his persecution of the church in Jerusalem, he next went to the High Priest for permission to persecute Jesus' disciples in Damascus (Acts 9.1-2). At this point no first-time reader of Luke's narrative would anticipate that Luke will later report that this same zealous persecutor of the Church becomes an equally zealous Spirit-filled prophet who goes about over land and sea to tell synagogue Jews of the Diaspora that Jesus is the fulfillment of their redemptive history (Acts 13.15-41); to tell Gentiles about God's grace toward them through creation (Acts 14.15-18) and to tell civilized Greeks that the unknown god has sent to them a man who will judge the world in righteousness (Acts 17.16-31).

Saul experiences this reversal from zealous persecutor to zealous Spirit-filled prophet while en route to Damascus to arrest disciples of Jesus and extradite them back to Jerusalem for imprisonment and judicial murder. This most dramatic turn around in the history of the early Church is effected through a Christophany. 'Suddenly', Luke reports, a 'light from heaven flashed around him...and [he] heard a voice saying to him, "Saul, why are you persecuting Me?"' (Acts 9.3b-4). As a symbol of his great spiritual blindness, the light from heaven blinded him, and his companions led him by the hand to Damascus (Acts 9.8). But the spiritual light which penetrated his religious consciousness soon resulted in physical sight, and, within days of arriving in Damascus he began proclaiming in the Jewish synagogues the message that Jesus is the Son of God, and the Christ (Acts 9.20, 22).

In those few days between Saul's arrival in Damascus and his preaching in the synagogues the essential foundation of his ministry is laid. At this time the Lord Jesus is preparing a certain disciple, Ananias, to search out and minister to Saul. The Lord informs him that Saul will, 'bear My name before the Gentiles and Kings and the sons of Israel' (Acts 9.15). This is programmatic for Paul's ministry (Acts 13–28). In addition, when Ananias comes to Saul he announces to him: 'the Lord Jesus...has sent me so that you may regain your sight, and be filled with the Holy Spirit' (Acts 9.17b). Thus, just as the disciples began their ministry having first been commissioned by the Lord (Acts 1.8) and then subsequently 'filled with the Holy Spirit' (Acts 2.4), so Saul will now begin his ministry, having also first been commissioned by the Lord (9.15) and then subsequently filled with the Holy Spirit (Acts 9.17). In other words, Saul begins his ministry in Damascus as a Spirit-filled prophet just as the disciples had earlier begun their ministry in Jerusalem empowered by the Spirit of prophecy.

1. *Paul: A Charismatic Apostle*

As he has done so often, beginning with his narrative about the acts of Jesus as the eschatological Spirit-anointed prophet, Luke once again employs the narrative strategy of inclusio to portray that Paul is a charismatic prophet from first to last. As we have just observed, through the agency of Ananias Saul is filled with the Holy Spirit at the onset of his ministry to bear the name of Jesus before Gentiles, kings and Israelites (Acts 9.15-17). His experience of being filled with the Spirit of prophecy is programmatic for his entire ministry. Indeed, the Holy Spirit is God's presence empowering Paul's ministry as charismatic prophet to Jews and Gentiles and to their respective leaders.

Throughout his ministry Paul the prophet has a broad range of experiences of the Holy Spirit. This range of experiences begins with his inaugural filling with the Spirit in Damascus (Acts 9.17). As with John the Baptist's earlier experience of being filled with the Spirit to be a prophet (Lk. 1.15, 76; 20.6), Paul is filled with the Spirit at this point to be a prophet (Acts 9.17, 13.1). To illustrate that Paul's experience of the Spirit is prophetic, Luke reports two subsequent examples. The first of these examples is at Paphos on the island of Cyprus. Here Paul, a true prophet (Acts 13.1), filled with the Holy Spirit, cursed Bar-Jesus/ Elymas, a Jewish false prophet (Acts 13.6-11). The second example is at Iconium where Paul and the other disciples 'were continually filled with joy and the Holy Spirit' (Acts 13.52). In contrast to the Paphos episode, where the term 'filled with the Holy Spirit' introduces a pneuma discourse of prophetic judgment, here at Iconium it describes a state of that joy, which is the fruit of the Spirit, and which is also reminiscent of that time when Jesus 'rejoiced greatly in the Holy Spirit' (Lk. 10.21). But, as foundational to Paul's ministry as prophet as this threefold experience of being filled with the Holy Spirit is, Paul has other experiences of the Spirit relating to the course of his ministry.

Luke not only reports that Paul was filled with the Holy Spirit three times (Acts 9.17; 13.9, 52), but he also frequently reports that Paul was led by the Holy Spirit. These experiences of being Spirit-led have two dimensions: the first concerning mission, and the second martyrdom. The Spirit leads Paul right from the outset of his mission. The Spirit, likely through an inspired prophet, initiates the mission to which the Spirit had already called them (Acts 13.2). This means that they have been sent out by the Holy Spirit (Acts 13.4). Paul is also led by the

Spirit in respect to where he will minister, that is, not in Asia or Bithynia, but from Troas to Macedonia (Acts 16.6-10). In addition to leading Paul for an effective and productive mission, the Spirit also leads Paul along the path of the rejected prophet toward his martyrdom. Thus, as the third evangelistic tour advances toward its conclusion, Luke reports that 'Paul purposed in the spirit [= Holy Spirit] to go to Jerusalem' (Acts 19.21). Not surprisingly, then, he testifies to the elders from the church at Ephesus that he is on his way to Jerusalem, inwardly 'bound in Spirit' (Acts 20.21), with the outward testimony of the Holy Spirit in every city (by Spirit-inspired prophets?) that bonds and afflictions await him (Acts 20.22). Luke reports two subsequent examples: at Tyre and at Caesarea (Acts 21.4, 11). In each episode, however, the Spirit-inspired prophets mistake what the Spirit is saying for a warning for Paul not to go up to Jerusalem, when, in fact, it is to prepare Paul in advance for the arrest and imprisonment which, in God's purpose, will happen to him after he arrives in the city. Thus, as Luke reports it, from Paul's departure from Antioch to begin his first evangelistic tour through to his arrival in Jerusalem to conclude his third evangelistic tour Paul repeatedly experiences the leading of the Holy Spirit.

2. *The Acts of Paul*

Luke reports that Paul and various companions conducted three evangelistic tours. Luke narrates all three of these evangelistic tours according to a common pattern or structure. First, each evangelistic tour begins with the report of one or more short introductory episodes which include a reference to the Holy Spirit. Secondly, Luke follows up these introductory episodes with a major report of Paul's ministry in one city (Pisidian Antioch, Philippi and Ephesus, respectively). Finally, Luke concludes his narrative with a series of summary reports about Paul's ministry in subsequent cities. The chart on p. 106 illustrates Luke's narrative strategy.

With rare exceptions Luke reports about the Holy Spirit only at the beginning of each evangelistic tour, not throughout the journey itself. These initial references to the Holy Spirit, therefore, are programmatic for the ministry which follows. Luke intends his reader(s) to understand that all of Paul's works and words which he reports are the works and words of a Spirit-filled, Spirit-led prophet. This observation about Luke's strategy is confirmed by the observation that references to the

Holy Spirit in the introductory episodes of the second and third evangelistic tours form an inclusio with the introductory references to the Holy Spirit in the first and second evangelistic tours, respectively.

Tour	Introductory Episodes	Major Report (Focus)	Series of Summary Reports
1	Emphasis is on the initiative of the Holy Spirit (13.1-3)	Pisidian Antioch (13.13-52)	Tour resumes and concludes in Antioch, with an aftermath in Jerusalem (14.1–15.30)
2	Emphasis is on the leading of the Holy Spirit (16.6-8)	Philippi (16.11-40)	Tour resumes and concludes in Antioch, with an appendix about Apollos (17.1–18.28)
3	Emphasis is on the gift of the Holy Spirit (19.1-7)	Ephesus (19.8-41)	Tour resumes and concludes in Jerusalem (20.1–22.21)

Luke's report about Paul's first evangelistic tour (Acts 13.1–14.28) clearly establishes the nature or character of these evangelistic tours. Luke shows that Paul and his companions go out and minister as prophets powerful in works and word. Specifically, they are prophets to the Jews of the Diaspora first and then prophets to the Gentiles. Luke demonstrates the prophetic character of the mission of Paul and his companions both directly and indirectly. As Luke begins his narrative the first fact which he reports is that the ministry team will consist of two, 'prophets and teachers', namely, Barnabas and Saul (Acts 13.1-2). Almost immediately Paul, the true prophet (Acts 13.1) finds himself to be opposed by a Jewish false prophet, Bar-Jesus (Acts 13.6). Luke reports how Saul, 'filled with the Holy Spirit' (Luke's technical term for prophetic inspiration, cf. Lk. 1.67; Acts 2.4, 17), pronounces judgment upon this false prophet, namely, blindness, which functions as a physical symbol of his spiritual blindness. Next, as delivered by one who is a prophet and teacher (Acts 13.1), whose mission is initiated by the Holy Spirit (Acts 13.2, 4), and who has recently been filled with the Holy Spirit (Acts 13.9), Paul's 'word of exhortation' in the synagogue at Pisidian Antioch (Acts 13.15-41) is a prophetic announcement that Jesus is the royal Son spoken about in the Scriptures. This conclusion is reinforced by the report which immediately follows that 'Paul and Barnabas spoke out boldly' (13.46). Earlier in Acts, both for the disciples and even for Paul himself, speaking boldly is the direct result of being filled with the Holy Spirit (Acts 4.31; 9.17, 27). Further, Paul and

Barnabas, speaking boldly, that is, under the Spirit's inspiration, assert that their mission is in continuity with the prophetic mission of servant Israel 'as a light for the Gentiles...bring[ing] salvation to the end of the earth' (Acts 13.47; Isa. 49.6). As Luke's readers will recognize, this also means that the prophetic mission of Paul and Barnabas is in continuity with the mission of the disciples as Spirit-empowered witnesses 'to the ends of the earth' (Acts 1.8). Clearly, throughout both the introductory episodes and the major report of the ministry of Paul and Barnabas at Pisidian Antioch, everything which Luke has reported is the ministry of Spirit-led and Spirit-filled charismatic prophets.

Luke's picture of Paul and Barnabas is the same in the concluding series of summary reports (Acts 14.1-28) as it was in the introductory episodes (Acts 13.1-3, 4-12) and the major report (Acts 13.13-52). These two peripatetic prophets continue to minister by works and by words which are empowered by the Holy Spirit. As persecuted and rejected prophets they leave Pisidian Antioch and travel southeastward to Iconium. Luke reports how that in Iconium 'the disciples [i.e. Paul and Barnabas] were continually filled with joy and with the Holy Spirit' (Acts 13.52). Luke next reports two typical results of being filled with the Holy Spirit: (1) they spoke out boldly (Acts 14.3a, cf. 4.31; 9.17, 27; 13.9, 46); (2) they performed unspecified but multiple 'signs and wonders' (Acts 14.3b). This means that their charismatic ministry in Iconium is similar to the earlier ministries of Jesus, the eschatological Spirit-anointed prophet (Acts 2.22), the disciples, eschatological Spirit-baptized prophets (Acts 2.43; 5.12), and the two 'full of the Holy Spirit' deacons, Stephen and Philip (Acts 6.8; 8.6, 13, respectively). Further, rejected and persecuted in Iconium (Acts 14.4, 5) as they had earlier been rejected and persecuted in Pisidian Antioch (Acts 13.50, 51), the two prophets flee to the city of Lystra. At Lystra they find a certain man who has been lame throughout his entire life (Acts 14.8). Not unexpectedly the prophet Paul heals him (Acts 14.9, 10). Thus, this healing of the lame man is the first reported example of the 'signs and wonders' performed by the Spirit-filled prophet, just as in Luke's narrative strategy the healing of the paralyzed man is one of the first examples of the Spirit-empowered ministry of Jesus (Lk. 4.14; 5.17-26), and the healing of the lame man at the temple Gate Beautiful is the first example of the many signs and wonders of the Spirit-filled prophets, Peter and John (Acts 2.4, 43; 3.1-11). Finally, Paul and Barnabas perform the hortatory function of prophets, 'encouraging' (παρακαλεῖν) the disciples in

Lystra, Iconium and Antioch (Acts 14.21, 23). This hortatory ministry
is, indeed, so characteristic of Paul's companion (e.g. Acts 11.23), that
he was earlier given the name 'Barnabas' which means this very thing:
Son of Encouragement, that is, Son of prophecy (υἱὸς παρακλήσεως,
Acts 4.36). And so, consistent with the picture of the prophets Paul and
Barnabas in the introductory episodes of this first evangelistic tour
(Acts 13.1-3, 4-12), and also with the picture in the major report (13.13-
52), in the series of summary reports Luke continues to report that Paul
and Barnabas minister as prophets who, like their charismatic predecessors, are prophets who are powerful in works and word.

If Paul's first evangelistic tour is a prophetic expedition both to Jews
of the Diaspora and to the Gentiles, then Paul's second and third tours
are similar prophetic expeditions. Having established so clearly and at
such great length that such is, indeed, the character of the first, Luke
gives only occasional reminders that this remains the case for the second and the third. He does this, for example, by showing that just as the
team on the first tour was made up of the leadership of two prophets,
Paul and Barnabas, and their companions, so the team on the second
tour is also made up of the leadership of two prophets, Paul and Silas
(Acts 15.32) and their companions. In addition, just as Luke began his
narrative of the first evangelistic tour of the two prophets with introductory episodes involving the Holy Spirit (Acts 13.1-3, 4-12), so he also
begins his narrative of the second evangelistic tour of the two prophets
with an episode involving the Holy Spirit. In this introductory episode
of the second evangelistic tour the prophets Paul and Silas are led by
the Holy Spirit (Acts 16.6-8) and by a complementary vision, a medium
of prophetic revelation (cf. Acts 2.17, Num. 12.6). Similarly, Luke's
report about the third evangelistic tour has an introductory episode
involving the Holy Spirit. On this occasion Paul is the agent by whom
about 12 disciples at Ephesus receive the Spirit of prophecy (Acts
19.6). Further, Paul continues to do one of the characteristic works of a
charismatic prophet, namely, to perform extraordinary miracles (Acts
19.11, 12). As earlier on the second evangelistic tour he continues to be
led by the Spirit (Acts 19.21; 20.22). At least twice, if not three times
this leading is via a prophetic word given by others (Acts 20.23; 21.4,
10). Finally, Paul does one of the most characteristic and dramatic of all
of the works done by charismatic prophets. He raises the dead (Acts
20.9, 10; cf. 1 Kgs 17.17-24; 2 Kgs 4.29-37, Lk. 8.49-59; Acts 9.36-
43). Therefore, though the evidence for the second and third evangelis-

tic tours is not as extensive as it was for the first evangelistic tour it is equally explicit and unambiguous. These tours are itinerant prophetic expeditions to Jews and Gentiles, and Paul continues to be a prophet whose works are empowered by the Spirit and whose words are inspired by the Spirit.

3. *Paul and Peter*

I have suggested that Peter, rather than Paul, is Luke's first and greatest hero of the early charismatic community. This suggestion is based on the observation that Peter's experience of the Holy Spirit and his prophetic ministry of Spirit-empowered works and words are the standard and the pattern for Luke's complementary portrait of both Paul's experience of the Holy Spirit and his prophetic works and words.

First, Peter's experience of the Holy Spirit is the pattern according to which Luke reports Paul's subsequent experience of the Spirit. For example, Luke first reports that either as a member of a group or as an individual Peter was 'filled with the Holy Spirit' three times (Acts 2.4; 4.8, 31). Luke subsequently reports that Paul, either as an individual or as a member of a group, is also 'filled with the Holy Spirit' three times (Acts 9.17; 13.9, 52). The following chart shows that they are not only 'filled with the Holy Spirit' three times but that they are 'filled with the Holy Spirit' according to the same pattern.

Apostle	Inaugural Filling	Pneuma Discourse	Filling of Quality	
Peter	Acts 2.4	4.8-12	4.31,	Holy Spirit and boldness
Paul	Acts 9.17	13.9-12	13.52,	Holy Spirit and joy

Luke's narratives about Peter and Paul make it amply evident that these two apostle-prophets were 'filled with the Holy Spirit' more often than the three examples by which Luke describes each of their characteristically Spirit-filled ministries. But the fact that Luke reports Paul's experience of the Spirit the same number of times as Peter's and according to the same pattern as Peter's shows that, for him, Peter's experience of the Spirit is the standard for Paul's experience.

Luke's report of Peter's experience of the Holy Spirit also extends to the leading of the Spirit for witness. For example, Peter is led to go to the Gentile God-fearer Cornelius by the direct instruction of the Holy Spirit (Acts 10.19, 20) and a complementary vision (Acts 10.9-16). Similarly, at the outset of Paul's second evangelistic tour a vision (Acts

16.9, 10) and the complementary leading of the Holy Spirit (Acts 16.6-8) directs Paul away from Asia and Bithynia to Troas and Macedonia.

In addition to Peter's being the standard of Paul's experience of the Holy Spirit, Peter's Spirit-empowered works are the model according to which Luke reports Paul's Spirit-empowered works. The following chart illustrates the parallels between the Spirit-empowered works of Peter and Paul.

Works of Power	Peter	Paul
Perform wonders and signs	2.43; 5.12	14.3
Heal lame men	3.1-10; 9.32-35	14.8-10
Healings effected by external instrumentality	5.15, 16 (Peter's shadow)	19.11,12 (Paul's aprons, handkerchiefs)
Agents for imparting Holy Spirit	8.15-17	19.6
Raise the dead	9.36-43	20.9-12

The use of the term 'signs and wonders' (Acts 2.43; 5.12; 14.3; 19.11) means that both Peter and Paul performed many more miracles than Luke reports examples of. But these examples of parallel Spirit-empowered works demonstrate that the Spirit-empowered works of the prophet Peter are the pattern according to which Luke subsequently presents Paul's Spirit-empowered works.

Luke not only parallels the Spirit-empowered works of these two charismatic prophets, Peter and Paul, but he also parallels some of Paul's Spirit-inspired words with some examples of Spirit-inspired words from Peter's earlier ministry. For example, Paul's pneuma discourse at Paphos ('filled with the Holy Spirit' [Acts 13.9] plus the report of direct speech [Acts 13.10, 11]) parallels Peter's earlier pneuma discourse before the Sanhedrin ('filled with the Holy Spirit' [Acts 4.8] plus the report of direct speech [Acts 4.9-12]). In addition, though Luke does not introduce them with his pneuma discourse formula, both Peter's witness to Cornelius (Acts 10.23-48) and Paul's word of exhortation in the synagogue at Pisidian Antioch (Acts 13.15-41) are Spirit-inspired words. This is indicated by two lines of evidence. First, programmatically, Jesus had announced to the disciples that their witness about him would be empowered by the Holy Spirit once they have received the Spirit (Acts 1.8) and both Peter and Paul have received this inaugural filling (Acts 2.4; 9.17). Secondly, by Luke's use of the narrative strategy of inclusio: Peter's witness is bracketed by adjacent references to the Holy Spirit (Acts 10.19, 44-48), and Paul's word of exhortation (Acts 13.15) = preaching (Acts 13.32) is also bracketed by references to the Holy Spirit (Acts 13.9, 52). Clearly, Luke intends Peter's witness and Paul's preaching, both of which follow the same sixfold pattern (see below), to be words inspired by the Holy Spirit.

Pattern	Peter	Paul
The gospel begins with John the Baptist	10.37	13.24, 25
Jesus ministers publicly	10.38	13.26
The Jews put Jesus to death	10.39	13.28, 29
God raises Jesus from the dead	10.40	13.30, 31
Affirmation of witness/preaching	10.41	13.32
Proof from prophecy	10.43	13.33-37

Peter's witness and Paul's preaching in words inspired by the Spirit complement their works empowered by the Spirit. This means that Luke's portrait of Peter as a prophet powerful in works and word is the standard for his subsequent portrait of Paul as a prophet powerful in works and word. It also means that Jesus, the eschatological Spirit-anointed prophet, powerful in works and word (Lk. 24.19) is the ultimate model by which Luke portrays these two Spirit-filled prophets.

In his narrative strategy, if Luke portrays Peter to be the model for Paul's experience of the Holy Spirit and his ministry as a prophet powerful in works and word, then, as a corollary, both Paul's experience and his prophetic ministry of works and word are the equal of Peter's. Therefore, as presented by Luke the parallels between Paul and Peter could mediate between two potentially rival factions in the early Church. To the Jewish Christians of Jerusalem and Judea, who might esteem Peter as an apostle and prophet more highly than Paul, Luke shows that Paul's charismatic ministry is the equal of Peter's. Similarly, to the largely cosmopolitan Diaspora Jewish and Gentile converts of Paul, Luke shows that the more provincial Peter had an antecedent ministry which is the equal of Paul's. In other words, whether in Judea or the far-flung reaches of the Roman Empire, both of these apostle-prophets are equally Spirit-filled, Spirit-led and Spirit-empowered.

4. *Paul's Churches: Prophetic Communities*

Applying the narrative strategy of inclusio Luke implies, but only twice makes explicit, that everywhere Paul preaches the gospel he establishes communities of Spirit-empowered prophets, just as the church in Jerusalem (Acts 2.1-17), the believers in Samaria (Acts 8.15-17) and the God-fearers who are centered in Cornelius's house at Caesarea (Acts 10.44-48) are communities of Spirit-empowered prophets. Luke first makes the prophetic character of Paul's churches explicit when he reports that at Iconium 'the disciples were continually filled with joy and with the Holy Spirit' (Acts 13.52), and that in the same city, 'many signs and wonders' were done by the hands of the two prophets, Paul and Barnabas (Acts 14.3). Luke makes the prophetic character of Paul's churches explicit for the second time when, many years later, Paul comes to Ephesus, finds and instructs some disciples, baptizes them, and then 'the Holy Spirit came upon them, and they began speaking with tongues and prophesying' (Acts 19.6). But between the opening report about the disciples at Iconium from the first evangelistic tour and the closing report about the disciples at Ephesus from the third evangelistic tour Luke is totally silent about any possible prophetic activity in the churches which this intrepid prophet and his companions established throughout the Aegean world.

Luke's silence about prophetic activity beyond what he has reported at Iconium and Ephesus is typical of his narrative strategy, rather than a fact about the absence of prophetic activity. Paul's letters to the churches that he established proves this. For example, when Paul writes to the churches of Galatia he asks three rhetorical questions about their experience of the Holy Spirit: '[D]id you receive the Spirit by the works of the Law?... Having begun in the Spirit are you now being perfected by the flesh?... Does he then, who provides you with the Spirit and works miracles among you, do it by the works of the Law, or by hearing with faith?' (Gal. 3.2-5). These rhetorical questions about their initial and ongoing experience of the Spirit complement Luke's own report about the twofold 'filled with the Spirit', and, 'signs and wonders', experience of the disciples at Iconium (Acts 13.52; 14.3). In addition, Paul reminds the church of the Thessalonians that 'the gospel did not come to you in word only, but in power and in the Holy Spirit...with joy in the Holy Spirit' (1 Thess. 1.5, 6). That the church in Thessalonica is a charismatic community of prophets is confirmed by Paul's twofold command: 'Do not quench the Spirit; do not despise prophetic utterances' (1 Thess. 5.19, 20). Luke's report about the ministry of the two prophets, Paul and Silas, in Thessalonica is totally silent about this powerful, joyous, prophetic dimension of the church there

(Acts 17.1-9). Finally, the same is true for Paul's ministry at Corinth. He boasts that the signs of a true apostle (i.e. signs, wonders and miracles) were done among them (2 Cor. 12.13). He concedes that the church which he founded at Corinth '[is] not lacking in any gift' (1 Cor. 1.7). He also observes that their exercise of these gifts is so undisciplined that when it comes to speaking in tongues and prophesying it is not done properly and in an orderly manner (1 Cor. 14.39, 40). Not surprisingly in light of his narrative strategy Luke is as silent about the prophetic character of the church at Corinth as he was earlier about the prophetic character of the church at Thessalonica.

The charismatic, prophetic character of the churches at Thessalonica and Corinth is equally the case in all of the churches which Paul, the charismatic prophet, established. When writing to the church at Rome he reports what Christ has accomplished through him 'in the power of signs and wonders, in the power of the Spirit' (Rom. 15.19). With two exceptions, Luke is totally silent about this Spirit-empowered ministry in the churches which Paul established. Though Luke is totally silent about most of this, his report about the disciples in Iconium and at Ephesus employing the narrative strategy of inclusio illustrates that from first to last the churches which Paul established were communities of charismatic prophets.

To sum up, Luke's report about Paul's experiences of the Holy Spirit is consistent with the experiences of the Spirit of the five charismatic prophets, especially Peter, about whom he has earlier reported (Acts 6.8–12.24). Luke reports that Paul is repeatedly 'filled with the Holy Spirit' (Acts 9.17; 13.9, 52). Luke identifies Paul as a prophet (Acts 13.1). He also reports that Paul does the typical works of his charismatic predecessors, namely, 'signs and wonders' (Acts 14.3)—including, but not limited to, healing the lame and raising the dead (Acts 14.8-11; 20.9-12). Clearly, like his charismatic predecessors, and like Jesus himself, Paul is a prophet powerful in works and words. Similarly, just as the disciples in Jerusalem and Caesarea are communities of prophets, so at Iconium and Ephesus, and, by implication, also at Thessalonica and Corinth, the churches which Paul established are also communities of prophets. As Luke gives no other picture for the acts of the charismatic community (Acts 2.42–6.7) or the acts of five charismatic prophets (Acts 6.8–12.24), so he gives no other picture of the acts of Paul (Acts 12.25–28.31). Paul is a prophet. His ministry is prophetic, and, from first to last, he establishes prophetic communities.

Chapter 7

THE PROPHETHOOD OF ALL BELIEVERS: A SYNTHESIS

In the previous chapters we have surveyed the unfolding of Luke's report about the prophethood of all believers. This began with him showing Jesus to be the eschatological anointed prophet (Lk. 24). In his Pentecost narrative he proceeded to show the transformation of Jesus' followers from a group of disciples to a community of Spirit-baptized prophets (Acts 1.1–2.41). After this he reported the acts of this fledgling community of prophets (Acts 2.42–6.7). Finally, and at length, Luke concluded his narrative by reporting about the acts of six charismatic prophets, from Stephen to Paul (Acts 6.8–28.31). In this chapter I shall synthesize these data about Luke's narrative theology of the prophethood of all believers. This is Luke's all-embracing, pervasive category for the people of God. This is true whether we open at the infancy narrative with its nationwide representative outburst of prophetic activity or whether we trace the evangelistic tours of the two teams of intrepid, itinerant prophets (Barnabas and Saul; Paul and Silas), who as the light to the Gentiles take the good news about Jesus to the ends of the earth.

1. Jesus is the Eschatological Anointed Prophet

To borrow the title from Dorothy L. Sayers' cycle of World War II radio plays, Luke introduces Jesus as 'The Man Born to Be King'. Specifically, the Lord God will give Mary's son, whom she is to name Jesus, the throne of his father David (Lk. 1.31-33). After three turbulent years of public ministry Jesus dies in Jerusalem as the rejected King (Lk. 23.33-49). But that is not the end of the story. The triumph of his public ministry is vindicated, and the tragedy of his rejection is reversed by his victorious ascension and enthronement (Acts 1.9-11; 2.32-35). Though he was born to be King and though he dies as rejected King, his entire public ministry, from his baptism by John in the Jordan through to his entry into Jerusalem, arrest, trial and crucifixion Jesus ministers as the eschatological Spirit-anointed prophet, namely, the Spirit-ful, Spirit-led and Spirit-empowered prophet. As the anointed prophet he sums up and fulfills at least five Old Testament prophetic traditions; he is variously, and in complementary fashion, the prophet like Isaiah, the prophet like Elijah and Elisha, like the rejected prophets, the royal prophet, and the prophet like Moses. In retrospect, some of his disciples identify him as 'a prophet mighty in works and word in the sight of God and of all the people' (Lk. 24.19). Thus, he is a charismatic prophet, healing the sick (e.g. the lepers, the blind), multiplying food, controlling nature—empowered by the Spirit in all of his works and words. He is the eschatological, Spirit-anointed prophet himself, and at the transition from his temporal prophetic ministry to his eternal royal ministry (Lk. 24–Acts 2), he transfers the Spirit of prophecy from himself to his disciples, thereby transforming them from a group of disciples to a Spirit-baptized community of prophets. In the vocational sense, when, on the day of Pentecost, Jesus pours out the Spirit of prophecy upon them, they become the sons of the prophet.

2. *Jesus' Followers are the Eschatological Community of Prophets*

Luke reports that immediately before Jesus ascended into heaven (Acts 1.9-11) to receive his royal enthronement (Acts 2.32-35), he commissioned his disciples to be witnesses about him from Jerusalem to Judea and Samaria and to the ends of the earth (Acts 1.8). To make them effective witnesses, they will, Jesus announces, receive power when the Spirit comes upon them (Acts 1.8). Luke reports that this happens when, on the day of Pentecost, Jesus pours out (Acts 2.36) the Spirit of prophecy (Acts 2.17-21), and they are 'filled with the Holy Spirit' (Acts 2.4). This experience of the Spirit is not only when they are empowered and filled with the Spirit, but also when they are baptized by the Spirit (Acts 1.5)—an experience of the Spirit which consecrates them for their vocation as witnesses. Therefore, as Luke reports it, the disciples, who are heirs and successors to Jesus' prophetic ministry, experience the Spirit much as Jesus himself did. In other words, just as the Spirit descended upon Jesus at the beginning of his ministry, so the Spirit is poured out upon the disciples at the beginning of their ministry (Lk. 3.22; Acts 2.33). In addition, just as Jesus was, therefore, full of the Holy Spirit, so the disciples are filled with the Holy Spirit (Lk. 4.1b;

Acts 2.4). And, just as Jesus was led by the Spirit, so the disciples will also be led by the Spirit (e.g. Acts 8.29; 10.19; 13.1-4; 16.6-8, etc.). Further, just as Jesus ministered in the power of the Spirit, so the disciples will witness in the power of the Spirit (Lk. 4.14; Acts 1.8). Finally just as the descent of the Spirit upon Jesus makes him the Spirit-anointed prophet, so the pouring out of the Spirit upon the disciples makes them the prophethood of all believers (Lk. 4.16-30; Acts 2.17-21). Therefore, it is as a prophetic community that the disciples minister in Jerusalem (Acts 2.42–6.7), that four prophets (Philip, Barnabas, Agabus and Peter) minister in Samaria, Judea and beyond (Acts 6.8–12.24), and that successive teams of prophets (Barnabas and Saul [Acts 12.25–15.35] and Paul and Silas [Acts 15.36–18.23]) take the good news about Jesus to the ends of the earth.

3. *The Community of Prophets is Empowered for Witness*

The pouring out of the Spirit of prophecy upon the disciples is primarily to empower them for their prophetic vocation as witnesses. Luke reports that the immediate result of having been baptized with the Spirit, empowered by the Spirit and filled with the Spirit (Acts 1.5, 8; 2.4) is that the disciples begin to witness. For example, on the day of Pentecost, as the aftermath to having the Spirit of prophecy poured out upon him, Peter solemnly testified (i.e. witnessed, διεμαρτύρατο) to the assembled, conscience-stricken crowd (Acts 2.40). Later, Luke reports, the apostles in Jerusalem witnessed to the resurrection of Jesus (Acts 4.32) and before the Council or Sanhedrin (Acts 5.32). This Spirit-empowered witness is not limited to Jerusalem but extends to Judea (e.g. Caesarea) when Peter, a prophet since Pentecost, witnesses to the Gentile Cornelius (Acts 10.39-42). These examples illustrate beyond dispute that the primary purpose of the pouring out of the Spirit of prophecy on the day of Pentecost is to empower the disciples for witness.

Therefore, just as Jesus was a prophet powerful in works and word (Lk. 24.19), so the disciples as witnesses are also prophets powerful in works and word. God attested to the Spirit-anointed, Spirit-ful, Spirit-led and Spirit-empowered ministry of Jesus as prophet with miracles, wonders and signs (Acts 2.22). Since the disciples are heirs and successors to Jesus' prophetic ministry and are empowered by the same Spirit that had earlier empowered Jesus, they also repeatedly and regularly perform wonders and signs. For example, Luke reports that in the aftermath to the Spirit of prophecy being poured out upon the disciples, 'many wonders and signs were taking place through the apostles' (Acts 2.43).

This becomes a typical, ongoing feature of their activity in Jerusalem (Acts 5.12). Just as the apostles performed signs and wonders in Jerusalem so other disciples, such as the Spirit-ful Stephen, performed great wonders and signs among the people in Jerusalem (Acts 6.8). Further, just as the disciples, whether apostles or deacons, performed wonders and signs in Jerusalem, so disciples, such as the Spirit-ful Philip, performed signs and great miracles in Samaria (Acts 8.6, 13). In addition, the prophetic team of Barnabas and Paul performed signs and wonders among the Jews and Gentiles (Acts 14.3; 15.12). Indeed, wherever Paul ministers among the Gentiles, God performs many extraordinary miracles (e.g. at Ephesus, Acts 19.11) as he had earlier done in Jerusalem and Samaria. Occasionally, Luke identifies some of these wonders and signs. For example, Peter and John heal a lame man in Jerusalem (Acts 3.1-10). Later, when traveling through western Judea, Peter once again heals a lame man and raises the dead (Acts 9.32-43). Luke identifies the signs and great miracles which Philip performed in Samaria to be the casting out of unclean spirits and the healing of the lame and the paralyzed (Acts 8.7). Luke identifies just one of the signs and wonders which the two prophets, Paul and Barnabas, performed. At Lystra they healed a man who had been lame from birth (Acts 14.8-12). Finally, at Ephesus the extraordinary miracles which Paul performed included healing the sick of their diseases and the casting out of evil spirits (Acts 19.11, 12).

Just as Jesus was a prophet who was powerful in words as well as in works, so, beginning with the day of Pentecost, the disciples are a community of prophets who are powerful in words as well as in works. Luke has prepared his readers to expect this because he has earlier reported that Jesus gave three different promises about this very thing. Specifically, he had promised that the Spirit would give his disciples words of defense (Lk. 12.12, 13), words of wisdom (Lk. 21.15) and words of empowered witness (Lk. 24.49; Acts 1.8). Luke also reports episodes when these promises are fulfilled. Thus, Jesus' promise that the Spirit would give his disciples words of defense is fulfilled in Peter's Spirit-filled pneuma discourse before the Sanhedrin (Acts 4.8-12). Similarly, the promise that the disciples would witness by words of

wisdom is fulfilled in Stephen's witness to the Hellenistic Jews in Jerusalem (Acts 6.10). Finally, the promise that the disciples would witness
with words empowered by the Spirit is fulfilled in Peter's pneuma discourse on the day of Pentecost (Acts 2.14-41). These three episodes of
promise-fulfillment are only examples of a wide range of Spirit-
empowered words which Luke reports in Acts.

As Luke reports it, the Spirit-empowered words which Jesus' followers speak include but are not limited to Spirit-empowered witness
(for example, not only does Peter witness on the day of Pentecost by
words empowered by the Spirit, but he later witnesses in Jerusalem,
Samaria and Caesarea with words empowered by the Spirit, either
explicitly [Acts 5.32] or by implication [(Acts 8.25; 10.39-41]). These
words inspired by the Spirit include that complex tongues-speak-
ing/praise/prophecy phenomenon which is the attesting sign of Spirit-
baptism (Acts 2.4, 11, 17, 18; 10.46; 11.15; 19.6). These Spirit-inspired
words also include not only Peter's Spirit-filled defense before the Sanhedrin but also Stephen's Spirit-ful defense before this same council
(Acts 6.5-7.55). Luke reports that typically when disciples are filled
with the Spirit they speak boldly (e.g. Acts 4.31; 9.17, 27). This range
of Spirit-empowered words includes a word of knowledge (Acts 5.3-9).
Spirit-ful disciples, such as Barnabas, speak words of encouragement or
exhortation (Acts 11.23, 24). Prophets, such as Agabus, make predic-
tions (Acts 11.27-30; 21.11). Moreover, the Spirit speaks through
prophets who initiate and direct mission (Acts 13.2; 20.23; 21.4). A
pneuma discourse may be a Spirit-filled word of judgment (Acts 13.9-
11). Finally, Luke reports that even the decision of the Jerusalem Council is inspired by the Spirit (Acts 15.28). Thus, the explicit range of
words inspired by the Spirit includes: (1) tongues-speaking/praise/
prophecy; (2) witness; (3) defense; (4) a word of knowledge; (5) encouragement or exhortation; (6) prediction; (7) direction; (8) judgment;
and (9) apostolic decree. This range of explicitly Spirit-inspired words
is also to be supplemented by all of Luke's reports about teaching and
preaching, since, invariably, it is Spirit-filled and Spirit-ful prophets
who do these activities.

Clearly, from first to last Luke reports that the disciples, apostles,
deacons and prophets who make up the eschatological community of
prophets are empowered by the Spirit for witness and a wide range of
other, complementary activities. Specifically, this community of
prophets is empowered for a wide, comprehensive range of works and

words. In this regard, the prophetic community and the Spirit-filled and Spirit-ful prophets who make it are the heirs and successors to Jesus, the eschatological anointed prophet, who was, himself, powerful in works and word.

4. *The Community of Prophets is Extended*

Following Jesus' program for the disciples's forthcoming Spirit-empowered witness which he has reported in Acts 1.8, Luke reports the geographic and implied ethnic spread of the gospel. The witness begins in Jerusalem (Acts 1–7), advances to Samaria and western Judea (Acts 8–12) and concludes with Paul's intrepid witness to the northwest sector of the 'ends of the earth' (Acts 13–28). The gospel not only spreads geographically, it also spreads ethnically. First, it spreads among the Jews of Jerusalem (Acts 1–7), western Judea (Acts 9.32-43), and to the Jews of the Diaspora (Acts 11.19-32; 13.4-43; 14.1-7; 17.1-15; 18.1-21; 19.8; 28.17-28). Next, as a result of the persecution which broke out when Stephen was martyred (Acts 8.1-4), Philip took the gospel to the Samaritans (8.5-13), where it found a joyous reception (Acts 8.8, 14). Finally, Philip (if the Ethiopian court official is a Gentile, rather than a Diaspora Jew [the most likely possibility]), Peter, and Barnabas and Paul take the gospel to the Gentiles (Acts 8.26-40; 10.1–11.18; 13.44-52; 14.8-28; 16.1-40; 17.16-34).

The agents who spread the gospel are, without exception, prophets. They are prophets by being either Spirit-filled (e.g. Peter, Paul) or Spirit-ful (e.g. Philip, Barnabas). Peter the Spirit-filled prophet witnesses in Jerusalem, Samaria and western Judea, and witnesses to Jews, Samaritans and Gentiles. Philip, the Spirit-ful prophet, who witnesses in Samaria and along the desert road, witnesses to Samaritans and to either a Diaspora Jew or Gentile God-fearer. Two successive teams of prophets, Barnabas and Paul, and Paul and Silas, respectively, preach the gospel to both Jews and gentiles throughout the Empire to the north and west of Antioch in Syria.

Not only are these Spirit-filled or Spirit-ful prophets the agents for the spread of the gospel, but they are also the agents for bestowing the gift of prophecy to new followers of Christ. Luke gives three examples of this. Peter is Luke's first and, perhaps, most important example. He is the agent through whom the Samaritan believers receive the Spirit (Acts 8.15-17) and during whose witness the Gentile, Cornelius, is baptized with the same Spirit of prophecy as the disciples had been baptized with on the day of Pentecost (Acts 10.44-48; 11.15-17). Luke also reports how many years later Paul is the agent by whom the disciples at Ephesus receive the same Spirit of prophecy as the disciples had earlier received on the day of Pentecost (Acts 19.6): they began speaking with tongues (compare Acts 2.4) and prophesying (cf. Acts 2.17). Luke's examples of the spread of the gift of prophecy are illustrative and representative rather than exhaustive and complete, for not only did the disciples at Ephesus receive the Spirit of prophecy, but the churches which Paul planted in Thessalonica and Corinth also received the Spirit of prophecy (1 Thess. 5.19, 20; 1 Cor. 12–14). Thus, Luke illustrates and Paul's letters to the churches confirm that the spread of the gift of the Spirit of prophecy is co-extensive with the spread of the gospel.

This spread of the Spirit of prophecy that is co-extensive with the spread of the gospel is consistent with the oracle of Joel which Peter applies to the pouring out of the Spirit on the day of Pentecost (Acts 2.14-21). At this time the descent of the Spirit transforms the company of disciples into a community of Spirit-filled prophets. But according to Joel this eschatological (or 'last-days') gift of prophecy is for all humankind (Acts 2.17). In the historical context of Joel's original prophecy the term 'all humankind' would have meant 'all Israel'. In the applied context of Pentecost it means 'all the repentant' (Acts 2.38, 39). Further, in the larger context of Acts it means 'all believers'—in Jerusalem (e.g. Acts 4.31), in Samaria and western Judea (Acts 8.15-17; 10.44-48), and to the 'ends of the earth' (e.g. Acts 19.6). Thus, Luke's narrative selectively but systematically shows that the spread of the gift of the Spirit of prophecy is co-extensive with the programmatic spread of the gospel. In other words, just as communities of disciples or believers are established in Jerusalem, Samaria and western Judea and throughout the Roman world, so the Spirit of prophecy is given so that these same communities in Jerusalem, Samaria and Judea and throughout the empire are communities of Spirit-filled, tongues-speaking prophets.

Luke reports how Spirit-filled, Spirit-ful prophets, such as Philip, Peter and Paul, take the gospel beyond Jerusalem to Samaria, Judea and the Roman Empire. Luke also reports that the spread of the gospel is initiated, led and/or sanctioned by the Holy Spirit himself. Luke narrates three examples when the Spirit speaks about direction in witness/ mission (whether he speaks directly or through a prophet we cannot always tell). Thus, to Philip the Spirit said, 'Go up and join the chariot' (Acts 8.29). Similarly, complementing a vision which Peter had just received, the Spirit said to him, 'But arise, go downstairs and accompany them [three messengers from Cornelius] without misgivings; for I have sent them myself' (Acts 10.19, 20). And to the group of prophets and teachers in Antioch the Holy Spirit said, 'Set apart for me Barnabas and Saul for the work to which I have called them' (Acts 13.1, 2). Later, the Holy Spirit, namely, the Spirit of Jesus, led Paul and Silas to Troas (Acts 16.6-8). Not unexpectedly, Luke selectively reports that the Spirit sanctions or endorses this spread of the gospel through Spirit-filled, Spirit-ful prophets. For example, the Spirit leads Peter to the Gentile Cornelius (Acts 10.19, 20), but God bore them witness by giving to them the Holy Spirit (Acts 15.8). Similarly, the Spirit initiates the evangelistic tour of Barnabas and Paul (Acts 13.2). This means that they have been sent out by the Holy Spirit (Acts 13.4). Therefore, the Spirit both initiates and sanctions the prophetic witness and mission to the Gentiles, which, in turn, establishes these converts as communities of prophets.

5. *Spirit of Prophecy or Soteriological Spirit?*

In Luke–Acts, that is, from the infancy narrative through to the prophet Paul's evangelistic tours, the Spirit is always the Spirit of prophecy. In Luke's pneumatology the Holy Spirit does not effect salvation (regeneration, initiation, incorporation) as he does in both the Johannine and Pauline pneumatologies. Nevertheless, Luke does bring the Spirit of prophecy into various relationships to salvation.

Luke reports several kinds of relationships between the Spirit and salvation. For example, because of the miraculous overshadowing agency of the Holy Spirit Mary conceives Jesus, who will be 'a Savior, who is Christ the Lord' (Lk. 2.11). Further, on the day of Pentecost Peter announces that salvation on the basis of repentance (Acts 2.38a, 40) is the prerequisite to receiving the same promised gift of the Spirit of prophecy as the disciples had just received (Acts 2.39; cf. 1.4, 5). Moreover, the gift of the Spirit-baptizing, tongues-speaking Spirit of prophecy which Cornelius and his household received (Acts 10.44-48; 11.15-17) is the witness that he (and, on the principle of historical precedent, all Gentiles) is saved apart from Judaizing circumcision (Acts 15.1, 8-11).

The examples of the Holy Spirit's role in the conception of Jesus, of Peter's promise of the gift of the Spirit to penitent Jews, and, finally, of the gift of the Spirit to Cornelius illustrate that the Spirit is brought into relationship to salvation in a variety of ways. No interpreter of Luke–Acts should be surprised by this. Since Luke–Acts is the story of the origin and spread of the gospel, and since the Spirit of prophecy is given to the penitent, it is historically and theologically impossible for there not to be a close relationship between salvation and the gift of the Spirit. But in spite of the close relationship between salvation and the gift of the Spirit, for Luke–Acts the *function* of the gift of the Spirit is not soteriological but prophetic. To confuse the close relationship between the two as meaning an identity of function is a serious methodological error and leads to a gross distortion of Luke's very clear and explicit pneumatology.

6. *Additional Functions and Effects of the Spirit*

The primary function of the Spirit of prophecy in Luke–Acts is to empower for witness. But though Luke–Acts is primarily about Spirit-empowered works and words, the Spirit of prophecy is not exclusively about service. Occasionally, Luke reports other functions and effects of the Spirit. For example, after the 70 disciples complete their mission and report back to Jesus, he 'rejoiced greatly in the Holy Spirit' (Lk. 10.20). Further, for both the disciples on the day of Pentecost and Cornelius and his household, the gift of the Spirit of prophecy results in tongues-speaking praise (i.e. speaking the great things of God, Acts 2.11; 10.46, cf. 19.6). In the Ananias and Sapphira episode, Peter's 'word of knowledge' purifies the church (Acts 5.1-11). At Antioch, the prophecy from the prophet Agabus about an impending famine results in a generous gift from the Christians there to the church in Jerusalem (Acts 11.27-30). At Iconium, Luke reports, the disciples are filled with joy and the Holy Spirit (Acts 13.52, cf. Lk. 10.20). Finally, either directly or through prophets the Spirit prepares Paul to face the bonds and afflictions which await him when he next arrives in Jerusalem (Acts 19.21; 20.22, 23; 21.4, 10, 11). In none of these examples is the Spirit of prophecy about witness. Rather, it is about praise, purity, joy, generosity and courage.

Though these praising, purifying, rejoicing effects of the Spirit of prophecy are just as valid as empowering for witness, Luke's reports about these effects is comparatively rare. His reports about these effects are rare, not because the Spirit of prophecy is irrelevant for this inner, non-evangelistic life of the Church, but simply because these effects are not Luke's primary focus. His primary focus is on witness, and, therefore, from first to last his narrative emphasizes the Spirit of prophecy as the empowering for witness.

7. *The Prophethood of All Believers: Contemporary Relevance*

Luke's doctrine of the people of God is that beginning in Jerusalem and co-extensive with the spread of the gospel they become the eschatological community of prophets—the prophethood of all believers. Luke's doctrine is not merely a matter of historical fact or inquiry. It is an urgent matter of contemporary relevance and reality.

The Church is to be a community of prophets. But from the post-apostolic period to the present it has not functioned as a prophetic community which is powerful in works and word. In fact, in too many places the Church views itself as a didactic community rather than as a prophetic community, where sound doctrine is treasured above charismatic action. Indeed, the preaching and teaching of the word displaces Spirit-filled, Spirit-led and Spirit-empowered ministry. The Spirit of prophecy has been quenched and the gifts of the Spirit have been sanitized and institutionalized. The non-Pentecostal/non-charismatic church needs to recapture its prophetic heritage, to which it is either hostile or indifferent.

As a prophetic community God's people are to be active in service. But all too often the Pentecostal, charismatic movements focus on the experience, the emotion and the blessing more than they do on Spirit-filled, Spirit-led and Spirit-empowered service. This shift in focus from vocation to personal experience, from being world-centered to self-centered, renders the service of the Pentecostal, charismatic movement just about as impotent as the service of the contemporary non-Pentecostal, non-charismatic church. This focus on experience rather than on service is like selling one's birthright of Spirit-empowered service for the pottage of self-seeking experience and blessing.

In the twentieth century there are many exceptions on both sides to these generalizations. But exceptions prove rather than falsify the rule. Therefore, in spite of the exceptions the above generalizations are sadly valid. The antidote to this malaise in which the Spirit of prophecy is either quenched or misused is for the contemporary Church to recapture, both doctrinally and vocationally, the first-century reality which Luke reports. This reality is one in which all of God's people are prophets because the Lord has put his Spirit on them. It is a reality where once again 'speaking with other tongues' is the physical symbol of a Spirit-empowered, worldwide witness. It is also a reality where Spirit-baptized believers are prophets powerful in works and word, both within the community and in the world.

But the contemporary Church will only function as the prophethood of all believers when the non-Pentecostal, non-charismatic church begins to teach Luke's doctrine of the people of God and when the Pentecostal, charismatic church more fully translates personal experience into Spirit-empowered words of witness and action. To the extent that this happens the acts of the prophetic community will be written afresh, and written in a greater way.

BIBLIOGRAPHY

Adamson, T., *The Spirit of Power* (Edinburgh: T. & T. Clark, 1985).

Arndt, W., *The Gospel According to St Luke* (St Louis: Concordia, 1956).

Arrington, F., *The Acts of the Apostles* (Peabody, MA: Hendrickson, 1988).

Aune, D.E., *The New Testament in its Literary Environment* (Philadelphia: Westminster Press, 1987).

—*Prophecy in Early Christianity and the Ancient Mediterranean World* (Grand Rapids: Eerdmans, 1983).

Barr, J., *The Semantics of Biblical Language* (Oxford: Oxford University Press, 1960).

Barrett, C.K., *The Holy Spirit and the Gospel Tradition* (London: SPCK, 1947).

—*Luke the Historian in Recent Study* (London: Epworth Press, 1961).

—*The Acts of the Apostles* (ICC; Edinburgh: T. & T. Clark, 1994).

Bruce, F.F., *Peter, Stephen, James and John: Studies in Early Non-Pauline Christianity* (Grand Rapids: Eerdmans, 1980).

—*The Book of Acts* (NICNT; Grand Rapids: Eerdmans, 2nd edn, 1988).

—*The Acts of the Apostles* (Grand Rapids: Eerdmans, 1990).

Bruce, R., *Secondary Prophecy as an Aspect of Luke's Charismatic Theology* (Portland: Grace Publishers, 1990).

Bruner, F.D., *A Theology of the Holy Spirit* (Grand Rapids: Eerdmans, 1970).

Burgess, S.M., and G.B. McGee (eds.), *Dictionary of Pentecostal and Charismatic Movements* (Grand Rapids: Zondervan, 1988).

Cadbury, H., *The Making of Luke–Acts* (London: SPCK, 1972).

Chance, J.B., *Jerusalem, the Temple and the New Age in Luke–Acts* (Macon, GA: Mercer University Press, 1988).

Conzelmann, H., *The Theology of St Luke* (New York: Harper & Row, 1960).

—*The Acts of the Apostles* (trans. J. Limburg, A.T. Kraabel and D.H. Juel; Hermeneia; Philadelphia: Fortress Press, 1987).

Deere, J., *Surprised by the Power of the Spirit* (Peabody, MA: Hendrickson, 1993).

Dunn, J.D.G., *Baptism in the Holy Spirit* (London: SCM Press, 1970).

—*Jesus and the Spirit* (London: SCM Press, 1975).

—'Baptism in the Holy Spirit: A Response to Pentecostal Scholarship on Luke–Acts', *JPT* 3 (1993), pp. 3-27.

Elbert, P. (ed.), *Essays on Apostolic Themes* (Peabody, MA: Hendrickson, 1985).

Ellis, E.E., *The Gospel of Luke* (NCB; London: Thomas Nelson, 1966).

—*Prophecy and Hermeneutic in Early Christianity* (Grand Rapids: Eerdmans, 1978).

Ervin, H., *Conversion-Initiation and the Baptism in the Holy Spirit* (Peabody, MA: Hendrickson, 1984).

—*Spirit-Baptism: A Biblical Investigation* (Peabody, MA: Hendrickson, 1987).

Evans, C., *Luke* (NIBC; Peabody, MA: Hendrickson, 1990).

Ewert, D., *The Holy Spirit* (Minneapolis: Augsburg, 1970).

Fee, G.D., 'Hermeneutics and Historical Precedent: A Major Problem in Pentecostal Hermeneutics', in R.P. Spittler (ed.), *Perspectives on the New Pentecostalism* (Grand Rapids: Baker Book House, 1976), pp. 118-32.

—*Gospel and Spirit: Issues in New Testament Hermeneutics* (Peabody, MA: Hendrickson, 1991).

—'Response to Roger Stronstad's "The Biblical Precendent for Historical Precedent"', *Paraclete* 27.3 (1993), pp. 11-14.

Fee, G.D., and D. Stuart, *How to Read the Bible for All its Worth: A Guide to Understanding the Bible* (Grand Rapids: Zondervan, 1982).

Fitzmeyer, J., *The Gospel According to St Luke* (AB, 28, 28A; Ann Arbor: Doubleday, 1985).

Gaffin, R., *Perspectives on Pentecost* (Philipsburg: Presbyterian Publishing, 1979).

Gasque, W.W., *A History of the Interpretation of the Acts of the Apostles* (Peabody, MA: Hendrickson, 1989).

Gee, D., *Pentecost* (Springfield: Gospel Publishing House, 1932).

Geldenhuys, N., *Commentary on the Gospel of Luke* (NICNT; Grand Rapids: Eerdmans, 1951).

Green, J.B., S. McKnight and I.H. Marshall (eds.), *Dictionary of Jesus and the Gospels* (Downers Grove, IL: InterVarsity Press, 1992).

Green, M., *Acts for Today* (London: Hodder & Stoughton, 1993).

—*I Believe in the Holy Spirit* (Grand Rapids: Eerdmans, 2nd edn, 1975).

Grudem, W., *The Gift of Prophecy in the New Testament and Today* (Westchester: Crossway Books, 1988).

Gunkel, H., *The Influence of the Holy Spirit* (Philadelphia: Fortress Press, 1979).

Haenchen, E., *The Acts of the Apostles* (trans. B. Noble and G. Shinn; Philadelphia: Westminster Press, 1971).

Hargreaves, J., *A Guide to Acts* (London: SPCK, 1990).

Hawthorne, G.F., R.P. Martin and D.G. Reid (eds.), *Dictionary of Paul and his Letters* (Downers Grove, IL: InterVarsity Press, 1993).

Hawthorne, G., *The Presence and the Power* (Dallas: Word Books, 1991).

Haya-Prats, G., *The Mighty Spirit of the Church* (Paris: Cerf, 1975).

Hemer, C.J., *The Book of Acts in the Setting of Hellenistic History* (Winona Lake, IN: Eisenbrauns, 1990).

Hengel, M., *Acts and the History of Earliest Christianity* (Philadelphia: Fortress Press, 1979).

Hill, D., *New Testament Prophecy* (Atlanta: John Knox Press, 1976).

Horton, S.M., *What the Bible Says about the Holy Spirit* (Springfield: Gospel Publishing House, 1979).

—*The Book of Acts* (RCNT; Springfield: Gospel Publishing House, 1981).

—*The Book of Acts* (CBL; Springfield: Gospel Publishing House, 1988).

Houston, G., *Prophecy: A Gift for Today?* (Downers Grove, IL: InterVarsity Press, 1989).

Hummel, C.E., *Fire in the Fireplace* (Downers Grove, IL: InterVarsity Press, 1978).

Hunter, H., *Spirit-Baptism: A Pentecostal Perspective* (Lanham, MD: University Press of America, 1983).

Israel, R.D., 'Joel 2.28-32 (3.1-5 MT): Prism of Pentecost', in C.M. Robeck, Jr (ed.), *Charismatic Experiences in History* (Peabody, MA: Hendrickson, 1985), pp. 2-14.

Jeremias, J., *Jerusalem in the Time of Jesus* (trans. F.H. and F.C. Cave; London: SCM Press, 1969).

Jervell, J., *Luke and the People of God: A New Look at Luke–Acts* (Minneapolis: Augsburg, 1972).

Keener, C.S., *The Spirit in the Gospels and Acts* (Peabody, MA: Hendrickson, 1997).

Keck, L.E., and J.L. Martyn (eds.), *Studies in Luke–Acts* (London: SPCK, 1968).

Krodel, G., *Acts* (Philadelphia: Fortress Press, 1981).

Lampe, G.W.H., *The Seal of the Spirit* (London: SPCK, 1967).

Lederle, H., *Treasures Old and New* (Peabody, MA: Hendrickson, 1988).

Lohse, E., 'πεντηκοστή', *TDNT*, VI, pp. 44-53.

Longenecker, R.N., *Biblical Exegesis in the Apostolic Period* (Grand Rapids: Eerdmans, 1975).

Ma, W., and R.P. Menzies (eds.), *Pentecostalism in Context: Essays in Honor of William W. Menzies* (JPTSup, 11; Sheffield: Sheffield Academic Press, 1997).

Maddox, R., *The Purpose of Luke–Acts* (Edinburgh: T. & T. Clark, 1982).

Marshall, I.H., *Luke: Historian and Theologian* (Grand Rapids: Zondervan, 1970).

—*The Gospel of Luke: A Commentary on the Greek Text* (NIGTC; Grand Rapids: Eerdmans, 1978).

—*The Acts of the Apostles: An Introduction and Commentary* (TNTC; Grand Rapids: Eerdmans, 1980).

—'The Present State of Lukan Studies', *Themelios* 14.2 (1989), pp. 52-57.

Martin, R.P., and P.H. Davids (eds.), *Dictionary of the Later New Testament and its Developments* (Downers Grove, IL: InterVarsity Press, 1997).

McGee, G., *Initial Evidence* (Peabody, MA: Hendrickson, 1991).

McQueen, L.R., *Joel and the Spirit: The Cry of a Prophetic Hermeneutic* (JPTSup, 8; Sheffield: Sheffield Academic Press, 1995).

Menzies, R.P., *The Development of Early Christian Pneumatology with Special Reference to Luke–Acts* (JSNTSup, 54; Sheffield: Sheffield Academic Press, 1991).

—'The Distinctive Character of Luke's Pneumatology', *Paraclete* 25.4 (1991), pp. 17-30.

—'Spirit and Power in Luke–Acts: A Response to Max Turner', *JSNT* 49 (1993), pp. 11-20.

—*Empowered for Witness: The Spirit in Luke–Acts* (JPTSup, 6; Sheffield: Sheffield Academic Press, 1994).

—'Luke and the Spirit: A Reply to James Dunn', *JPT* 4 (1994), pp. 115-38.

Menzies, W., *Anointed to Serve* (Springfield: Gospel Publishing House, 1971).

Minear, P.S., *To Heal and to Reveal: Prophetic Vocation According to Luke* (New York: Seabury, 1976).

Montague, G., *The Holy Spirit* (Paulist Press, 1976).

Moody, D., *Spirit of the Living God* (Philadelphia: Fortress Press, 1968).

Morris, L., *Spirit of the Living God* (London: Inter-Varsity Press, 1960).

—*Luke* (TNTC; Leicester: Inter-Varsity Press, 1988).

Moulton, J.H., and G. Milligan, *The Vocabulary of the Greek New Testament Illustrated from the Papyri and Other Non-Literary Sources* (Grand Rapids: Eerdmans, 1963).

Neil, W., *The Acts of The Apostles* (NCB; London: Oliphants, 1973).

Nolland, J., *Luke* (WBC; Dallas: Word Books, 1989).

Ogilvie, L., *Acts* (Waco, TX: Word Books, 1983).

O'Neill, J., *The Theology of Acts in its Historical Setting* (London: SPCK, 1970).

O'Toole, R., *The Unity of Luke's Theology: An Analysis of Luke–Acts* (Wilmington, DE: Michael Glazier, 1984).

Plummer, A., *A Critical and Exegetical Commentary on the Gospel According to St Luke* (ICC; Edinburgh: T. & T. Clark, 1922).

Polhill, J.B., *Acts* (NAC; Nashville: Broadman Press, 1992).

Powell, M.A., *What Are They Saying about Acts?* (New York: Paulist Press, 1991).

Riches, J., *The Purpose of Luke–Acts* (Edinburgh: T. & T. Clark, 1982).

Robeck, C.M., Jr (ed.), *Charismatic Experiences in History* (Peabody, MA: Hendrickson, 1985).

Robertson, A.T., *Luke the Historian in the Light of Research* (repr.; Grand Rapids: Baker Book House, 1977).

Schweizer, E., *The Holy Spirit* (London: SCM Press, 1980).

—*The Good News According to Luke* (Atlanta: John Knox Press, 1984).

Shelton, J.B., *Mighty in Word and Deed: The Role of the Holy Spirit in Luke–Acts* (Peabody, MA: Hendrickson, 1991).

Spittler, R., *Perspectives on the New Pentecostalism* (Grand Rapids: Baker Book House, 1976).

Stanton, G., 'Stephen in Lucan Perspective', in E.A. Livingstone (ed.), *Studia Biblica 1978*. III. *Papers on Paul and Other New Testament Authors* (JSNTSup, 3; Sheffield: JSOT Press, 1980).

Stein, R., *Luke* (NAC; Nashville: Broadman Press, 1992).

Stott, J.R.W., *Baptism and Fullness* (London: Inter-Varsity Press, 1975).

—*The Spirit, the Church and the World* (Downers Grove, IL: InterVarsity Press, 1990).

Stronstad, R., 'The Influence of the Old Testament on the Charismatic Theology of St Luke', *Pneuma* 2.1 (1980), pp. 28-50.

—*The Charismatic Theology of St Luke* (Peabody, MA: Hendrickson, 1984).

—'The Hermeneutics of Lucan Historiography', *Paraclete* 22.4 (1988), pp. 5-17.

—'The Holy Spirit in Luke–Acts', *Paraclete* 23.1 (1989), pp. 8-13.

—'The Holy Spirit in Luke–Acts', *Paraclete* 23.2 (1989), pp. 18-26.

—'The Biblical Precedent for Historical Precedent', *Paraclete* 27.3 (1993), pp. 1-10.

—'Affirming Diversity: God's People as a Community of Prophets', *Pneuma* 17.2 (1995), pp. 145-57.

—*Spirit, Scripture and Theology: A Pentecostal Perspective* (Baguio City, Philippines: APTS Press, 1995).

Stronstad, R., and L. Van Kleek, *The Holy Spirit in the Scriptures and the Church* (Clayburn: WPBC, 1987).

Talbert, C.H., *Literary Patterns, Theological Themes and the Genre of Luke–Acts* (Missoula, MT: Scholars Press, 1974).

—*Reading Luke: A Literary and Theological Commentary on the Third Gospel* (New York: Crossroad, 1982).

Tannehill, R., *The Narrative Unity of Luke–Acts* (Philadelphia: Fortress Press, 1986).

Tiede, D. *Prophecy and History in Luke–Acts* (Philadelphia: Fortress Press, 1980).

Turner, M., *Power from on High: The Spirit in Israel's Restoration and Witness in Luke–Acts* (JPTSup, 9; Sheffield: Sheffield Academic Press, 1996).

—' "The Spirit of Prophecy" as the Power of Israel's Restoration and Witness', in I.H. Marshall and D. Peterson (eds.), *Witness to the Gospel: The Theology of Acts* (Grand Rapids: Eerdmans, 1998), pp. 327-48.

Williams, C.S.S., *The Acts of the Apostles* (HNTC; Peabody, MA: Hendrickson, 1964).

Williams, D., *Acts* (NIBC; Peabody, MA: Hendrickson, 1985).

Willimon, W., *Acts* (Atlanta: John Knox Press, 1988).

INDEXES

INDEX OF REFERENCES

OLD TESTAMENT

NEW TESTAMENT

INDEX OF AUTHORS

JOURNAL OF PENTECOSTAL THEOLOGY

Supplement Series

1 PENTECOSTAL SPIRITUALITY: A PASSION FOR THE KINGDOM
   Steven J. Land
   pb ISBN 1 85075 442 X

2 PENTECOSTAL FORMATION:
   A PEDAGOGY AMONG THE OPPRESSED
   Cheryl Bridges-Johns
   pb ISBN 1 85075 438 1

3 ON THE CESSATION OF THE CHARISMATA:
   THE PROTESTANT POLEMIC ON MIRACLES
   Jon Ruthven
   pb ISBN 1 85075 405 5

4 ALL TOGETHER IN ONE PLACE:
   THEOLOGICAL PAPERS FROM THE BRIGHTON CONFERENCE
   ON WORLD EVANGELIZATION
   Harold D. Hunter and Peter D. Hocken (eds.)
   pb ISBN 1 85075 406 3

5 SPIRIT AND RENEWAL:
   ESSAYS IN HONOR OF J. RODMAN WILLIAMS
   Mark Wilson (ed.)
   pb ISBN 1 85075 471 3

6 EMPOWERED FOR WITNESS: THE SPIRIT IN LUKE –ACTS
   Robert P. Menzies
   pb ISBN 1 85075 721 6